THE SECRET OF PLANTS IN THE ENVIRONMENT

RISHIKESH UPADHYAY

INDIA • SINGAPORE • MALAYSIA

Notion Press

Old No. 38, New No. 6
McNichols Road, Chetpet
Chennai - 600 031

First Published by Notion Press 2020
Copyright © Rishikesh Upadhyay 2020
All Rights Reserved.

ISBN 978-1-64850-920-9

This endeavour is dedicated to

The memory of his father, Late PITAMBER UPADHAYA,
and for investing his gesture of heart upon his mother,
Smt. NANDAKALA (Bawni) UPADHAYA
and sister, Ms. SANDHYA UPADHYAY

Contents

Acknowledgements

The author records his heartfelt thanks to all those individuals, their surperb views, including grammatical alerts, for improvement of the glitches, proofreading, criticisms, useful tips, constructive comments, plagiarism and other suggestions.

He would like to communicate his appreciation to his students, past and present, in the Department of Botany, Haflong Government College affiliated with Assam University, India for their helpful comments and stimulating conversation.

His gratitude is also due to those individuals or persons whose names have not been mentioned herein the acknowledgements, but whose views have directly or indirectly been highly beneficial in the presentation.

He would like to thank and greet S. Shruthi, Grace and V. Menon of Notion Press Publication, for their efforts from shaping to bringing out his book to the hands of the esteemed readers.

And finally, he profoundly recognizes the support of his brothers and sisters whose constant helps and blessings for every success in his endeavour have made this presentation possible in the hands of the esteemed readers.

Thank you.

Author's Note

Plants are the fundamental aspects of our biosphere. In nature, plants may be exposed during their ontogeny to a wide variety of favourable or harmful stress factors or environmental changes. The growth, behaviour and variations of plants in response to various environmental stresses differ in different plants; they are modified in the same species by the climate and surroundings to which the plants become habituated. Several phenomena of daily or diurnal periodicity in plant are known, but the relationships between the two are more or less obscure. Due to the gravitational stimulus, the roots of plants move downwards and the shoots upward; the sprouts are directly affected by natural environmental changes from the initial growth of plants to their maturity.

This book is an outcome of the painstaking acquisition of knowledge, experience and learning regarding plants and their relative environments that inspired the author during the course of teaching and performing research. The book intends to provide a synthesis of knowledge on the adaptation pathways induced by environmental changes or stressors, such as drought, chemical agents, electric stimulus, mechanical stress, magnetic fields, flash-flooding, submergence, biotic stress, waterlogging, mineral nutrients, freezing, radiation stress, high salinity, temperature fluctuations, pollution, heat, heavy metal stress and light stress.

List of illustrations

Prologue

This plant represents what's happening inside of you. The world, like the soil, is cold and dark - layered with a history of destruction and death. You were planted in this world to rise above it. Do you not see? The very existence of this darkness gives you the opportunity to become a light to the world.

– Seth Adam Smith,
"Rip Van Winkle and the Pumpkin Lantern"

The quality of our life depends on the quality of the surrounding environment. Photosynthesis is central to all aspects of plant biology as the provider of energy and assimilates for growth and reproduction, but how it is regulated by abiotic stresses, such as salinity and water deficits, and by biotic stresses, such as insect herbivory, has not been determined. In some cases, plants communicate with their tissues and organs to synchronize their responses to changing natural environments. As plants lack a central nervous systems, their sensing and communicating mechanisms are slightly different from animals. Understanding the physiology of stress, either biotic or abiotic, or different environmental changes in plant growth and development, are important to many environmentalists and plant scientists because physical stress has a prominent impact on biological diversity and agricultural productivity, as well as other environmental and ecological maladies in nature.

As sessile organisms, plants must cope with different environments, such as soil salinity, drought, and extreme temperatures. Plants have developed suitable mechanisms to adapt to these environments during their long evolutionary history. In response to stressful conditions imposed by their environment, which could affect growth and development throughout the plant life cycle, plants must be able to perceive, process, and translate different stimuli into adaptive responses. Knowledge about the plant stress response is vital for the development of breeding and biotechnological strategies to improve stress tolerance in crops and, consequently, crop yields. Curtailing crop losses due to various environmental stressors is a significant area of concern to cope with the increasing food requirements. Proteins are essential constituents of the cell that are easily damaged under environmental stress condition. There is a degree of inherent circularity in the definitions of the terms stressor, stress and stress response, and part of the confusion surrounding these concepts may arise from a lack of precision in the distinctions between them and the word stress. Thus, pressure is often used somewhat loosely to refer to both environmental factors causing its response. Stressors are environmental factors that cause stress in plants. Stressors include biotic factors, such as food availability, the presence of predators, infection with pathogenic organisms or interactions with conspecifics, as well as abiotic factors, such as temperature, water availability and toxicants. Responses to stress are thought to ensure short-term protection of plants followed by the formation of specific adaptation mechanisms. An extensive study on oxidative stress has demonstrated that exposure of plants to adverse environmental conditions induces overproduction of ROS, such as superoxide radical ($O_2\cdot$), (H_2O_2) and hydroxyl radical (OH), in plant cells [1]. As a consequence, plants have evolved cellular adaptive responses such as the upregulation of oxidative stress protectors and accumulation of protective solutes. Among the non-enzymatic antioxidants, ascorbate is found to be one of the best-characterized compounds, required for many vital metabolic functions in plant cells. Ascorbate acts as an antioxidant, protecting cells against oxidative stress. Ascorbic acid can eliminate different ROS, including singlet oxygen, superoxide and hydroxyl radicals.

Stress genes activation

Transcription factors

ROS Signalling

Upset ion homeostasis

Oxidative Stress induction

Plant Environmental Stress

1.   General responses of plant to Environmental Stress.

CHAPTER ONE

Appliance of Plants

All human affairs follow nature's great analogue, the growth of vegetation. There are three periods of growth in every plant. The first, and slowest, is the invisible growth by the root; the second and much accelerated is the visible growth by the stem; but when root and stem have gathered their forces, there comes the third period, in which the plant quickly flashes into blossom and rushes into fruit. The beginnings of moral enterprises in this world are never to be measured by any apparent growth... At length comes the sudden ripeness and the full success, and he who is called in at the final moment deems this success his own. He is but the reaper and not the labourer. Other men sowed and tilled and he but enters into their labours.

— Henry Ward Beecher, *"Life Thoughts"*

Even if we do not have all of the answers regarding areas with the potential to receive rainfall, we can be sure that there will be rain if plants are present. Downpours occur in forest or plantation areas at least once in twelve months. One cannot exactly state how the relationship between nature and forest areas developes; for example, it requires more than clairvoyance to determine the truth about the relationship between the human race and nature. The exact mechanism seems to be complex because of the vastness of the term nature. The more that researcher describes it subjectively, the more it becomes exhaustive, for the term holds relative importance everywhere. In this context, air, water and soil represent the primordial needs of all living beings, including plants, upon which we will expatiate.

The plants in our environment present a majestic greenness that attracts both humans and animals with respect to different tastes.

However, it is known that the presence of trees in soil ensures the restriction of erosion problems.

Retaining the aforementioned perspective, we established a series of objectives regarding the scrupulous use of soil and water via the adaptation of eco-friendly measures.

First, we motivate people towards the adaptation of alternative methods of production via the implementation of scientifically viable schemes to raise the economic conditions of the poor people in the Dima Hasao District.

Second, we place more emphasis on eliminating old habits by introducing the Cash Crop Development Scheme, which consists of rubber, tea, cardamom, and broom plantations, among others, as a substitute for food production for their livelihood.

Additionally, in the course of implementing the afforestation plantations, the government of India suggested the convergence of agriculturale crops towards the introduction horticulturale plantations, such as ginger, turmeric, papaya, lemon and dagger plants (*Agave Americana*) under the existing plantations of rubber. The convergence helps erect a vegetative barricade for gazers, as well as for illegal felling of trees in departmental afforestation. The aim of the literary erection of the fence is to attract people who, in turn, will help check the regular felling of trees from plantation fields.

Moreover, the convergence ensures some financial returns for the villagers who adopt it in the plantation fields.

Apart from the two types of plantations in one field as described above, we have also planted ornamental plants in and around our residential areas.

For the protection of soil, such measures as bench terracing, land reclamation, and gully control works have been adopted for the conversion of the abandoned land after shifting cultivation by the villagers of the hilly regions of Assam. These schemes attempt to help cultivators adopt wet cultivation.

Furthermore, there are water bodies everywhere at their location site.

The plantations that have no human control may well be described as forests, which can be classified into two types – reserved and unreserved. The former case, remains under the regular control of the forest department for the preservation of the flora and fauna of the particular areas selected for carrying out the particular role by the particular department of the concerned government; in contrast, the unreserved forests remain under the control of the state land, revenue and settlement department.

The protection of living beings ensures the protection of the environment from hazards, and, in the same way contains the erosion to control the depletion of forests.

To evaluate the scarcity of water, we assess the degradation of forests, for which the Government of India's recently launched the water conservation mission, which is popularly known as *Jal Shakti Abhiyan,* in which the implementation of vigorous plantations of saplings has been conducted. This mission will certainly help to streamline the protection of ecological and environmental imbalances.

Such plantations ensure the tightening of loose soil, which, in turn, prevents runoff water from the rainy season from washing away the topsoil that causes erosion. The losses of fertile soil also cause excess exposure of rocks underneath the soils, generating unbearable weather conditions for the denizens of the Earth.

What is soil? When we think about soil, we begin to use and think of it throughout our conscious and unconscious movements. Our entire movement on the outer surface of soil is also known as Earth.

From our footing to sleeping on our beds via the support of wooden or iron coats, the role of the outer surface of soil, which is also known as Earth, is present from our birth to our death. Considering the wonder of the adaptation of human lives to Earth, we humans conferred the Knight of the Mother to the outer surface of soil.

Since we need air and water for life on Earth, better treatment of the outer surface of soil is indispensably necessary to ensure natural air and water in our planetary life.

As the green coverage of soil dwindles due to the wanton destruction of forests, as well as to conflagration, the original sources of streams and rivers are naturally bound to either become saturated or threatened, portending the slow and steady decline of the water tank below the lower surface.

Commenting on the purpose of our life in the universe, Dr. Albert Einstein once said, "If the universe is an accident, we are accidents. However, if there is meaning in the universe, there is meaning in us also"

Based on the same syllogism, let us presume that all living beings have a purpose of life on Earth. Although it is not possible for everyone to simultaneously determine who or what is born for what purpose on Earth, it is clear that every living being has a purpose and or right to live in the universe – for instance, if someone is devoted to creation, another is actively engaged in destruction; if one is good, the other is evil; if one is a saint, the other is a sinner; if one is a meat eater, the other is a vegetarian, etc. Hence, no one can imagine any permanent destruction of the other based on the principle of our performance, although efforts are sometimes exerted out of expediency.

The wanton destruction of forests not only deprives the existence of green habitats, but also the wildfires that spread from the fields of shifting cultivation wreak havoc with the lives - and visible properties in the case of the human race - of all living beings in particular regions of conflagration.

Regardless of agreement about the matter, when the right to existence of others is eliminated, we extricate the role of an individual from his share of equal contribution towards a peaceful co-existence between humans and other living beings, thereby violating our own conscience of protecting ecology for a better environment.

In view of the rapid growth of the human population, the use of land, or, for that matter soil, becomes haphazard. As long as our need for land is limited, the danger of erosion becomes serious. For our benefit, we use the soil according to our personal needs, and not for the overall benefits of all people in our environment.

To streamline the same phenomenon, it is presumed that it actually leads to the birth of the need for the formation of think tanks at international, national and state levels. In addition, its creation for the necessity of framing certain rules ensures a safer earth. In the aftermath of erosion caused by the loss of alluvial soils, the rise of riverbeds becomes inevitable following the deposition of the washed away particles by the runoff water from the rainy season.

It may be stated that the need to preserve the environments of human beings has already been felt by conscientious people. However, in implementing remedial measures, our mission towards protecting these environments has in turn changed or our efforts have often not been given the chance to bear fruit, precisely because of the lack of strong determination or resolution.

The rise of river basins causes floods that wreak havoc with the lives and properties of humans in Plains areas.

Further, there is a standing problem of shifting cultivation in some tribal belts in India, where the system of growing food for livelihood consists of large-scale destruction, as well as burning of pristine forests.

Following the wanton burning after the felling of trees from unclassified forests, farmers uproot stumps from their cultivation land. The result of the displacement of stumps of cut trees leads to loosening of the soil, enabling the rain water to sweep away all fertile soils from low-laying areas.

In this context, the good governance motivates farmers to adopt a settled cultivation, which is popularly known as wet cultivation, for which some measures, such as bench terracing and contour bounding, have been introduced in the field to meet the basic requirements for implementing the schemes.

In short, all our activities pertaining to the protection of the environment directly or indirectly emerge from the need to grow plants for the survival of humans and other living beings. When planting trees, various kinds of stress are experienced by the plants. Having dwelt on the importance of plants for living beings, we turn to the study of the management of stress or environmental changes in plants.

CHAPTER TWO

Plants and Temperature Change

If it was the warmth of the sun, and not its light, that produced this operation, it would follow, that, by warming the water near the fire about as much as it would have been in the sun, this very air would be produced; but this is far from being the case.

– Jan Ingenhousz, *"Experiments upon vegetables"*

Temperature fluctuations strongly influence plant growth and biomass formation. In nature, the upper part of the plant is exposed to the temperature of the air, while the root underground is exposed to a very different temperature. A sudden variation in temperature often acts as an excitatory shock to plants, which gives rise to sudden fluctuations in growth. It changes or amends the plasma membrane, ultimately changing its structural and functional aspects and the expression of genes. A deviation from average temperature conditions causes a destabilization of the metabolic processes of plant species. When exposed to stresses caused by various factors, including heavy metals, temperature or high salt levels, the balance is altered, leading to a series of changes in metabolic processes related to stress acclimation, development, or programmed cell death (Gechev et al.

2006). Growth rates generally increase where the temperature is limiting and decrease where water is healthy. Higher temperatures will probably accelerate mineralisation of soil organic matter, intensifying soil constraints (Lynch and St. Clair 2004). In turn, these factors can limit root penetration and plant development. Drought stress can interact with higher temperatures, or with poor soil fertility, which limits root development. Identifying the critical interactions and incorporating them into a selection programme is perhaps the most challenging aspect of improving adaptation to abiotic stress factors. Stresses caused by adverse environmental conditions are responsible for substantial economic losses of pea crops, such as drought, high/low temperatures, and salinity, representing essential abiotic constraints. The extent of the yield losses depends mainly on the intensity, duration and distribution of the adverse conditions. For instance, water requirements for pea are relatively high, particularly during germination and flowering. Thus, water limitations at flowering lead to a shorter flowering period and the abortion of flowers (Ney et al. 1994). Breeding programmes are therefore conducted to release winter hardy cultivars that are able to survive freezing temperatures and other associated winter stresses. The majority of the plants survive at high temperatures through the avoidance and alleviation of overheating and due to the ability of the protoplasm to bear these temperatures (Larcher 1995).

Underwater and salinity stress and the uptake of water and minerals are disturbed; hence, photosynthetic activity decreases. Photosynthesis is well known to be sensitive to heat stress (Berry and Bjorkman 1980). Additionally, the accumulation of soluble sugars in leaves during a low-temperature treatment preceding frost under controlled conditions has been reported (Bourion et al. 2003). The transduction chains for high and low temperature signals do not seem to partly cover or share common elements (Sung et al. 2003), though cell membranes appear to play a function in plant responses to either temperature extreme.

In general, promising traits to be analysed for drought tolerance are shoot and root morphology and developmental pattern, small-scale anatomies such as stomata features, physiological characteristics belonging to osmotic adjustment or water use efficiency and related items. In temperate and semi-arid climates, rapid development generally decreases the drought penalty. Drought considerably diminishes antifertility, thus reducing options to escape by speedy development (Stoddard 1986). Leaf temperature depression was found to be negatively and significantly correlated to stomatal conductance and transpiration rate ($0.59 < r < 0.85$) and positively correlated with intrinsic water use efficiency ($r = 0.75$ in the dry set and $r = 0.51$ in the wet game) under non-stress conditions. The sensitivity of the IAA transport mechanism (s) to different temperatures may be responsible for the dissimilarity in kinetics of growth allocation during phototropism from 15 °C to 25 °C. The lower temperature could upset the rate of transport of auxin along and across the hypocotyls and thus delay the reply of tissue to inward auxin and reduce the rate of phototropic bending.

Examining the effect of experimental drought stress on these faba beans, Khazaei et al. (2013) reported an increase in stomata density and a decrease in size, accompanied by an expected reduction in gas exchange. Temperature also induces changes in the conformational structure of membrane proteins, disturbing calcium ion fluxes and metabolic reactions. Increases in stomatal density may be partly caused by the drought-induced decrease in leaflet size. The stomatal frequency and size show a definite negative, genetic correlation, counterbalancing each other's presumed effects on drought tolerance. Hence, stomatal opening and closing behaviours and features such as root and cuticle traits must have a marked impact on the drought tolerance of faba bean. Whether adaptation to drought causes a general increase or decrease in stomatal frequency and size do not yet to be fully resolved to date. Indeed, leaf temperature depression as a direct result of transpiration is promising to reflect water use efficiency and stomatal conductance in faba bean (Khan et al. 2007). Temperature differences are mainly meaningful under non-stress conditions, but under stress, with presumably all stomata closed, differences are insignificant, depending on the severity of the pressure applied. Given the lack of markedly drought-tolerant faba bean accessions, alien genes should be introgressed from other crops. The rise in high temperatures can also reveal a way to maintain the three-dimensional structure required for the correct function of enzymes or structural cellular components, thus leading to the loss of proper enzyme structure and activity. Misfolded proteins often aggregate and precipitate, creating severe problems inside the cell.

Trees provide both particulate matter and temperature mitigation. Temperature is one of the most critical environmental factors affecting the seasonal growth and geographic distribution of plants. The increased occurrence of high temperatures worldwide is a primary global concern, as they dramatically affect plant yields. Upon increasing temperature exposure, plants sense the temperature change and initiate cellular and metabolic responses that enable them to adapt to their new environmental conditions. Hence, the rising temperatures around the world will affect the life cycle of plants by promoting seed germination, reducing vegetative growth, promoting early flowering, and disrupting the seasonal growth of certain species (Fitter and Fitter 2002). Reduced photosynthesis because of increased temperature can in part be ascribed to Rubisco deactivation (Crafts-Brandner and Salvucci 2000). A clear concept of the mechanisms by which plants acquire thermotolerance is therefore essential, as it facilitates the development of high-temperature tolerant plants through molecular marker-assisted breeding techniques. Recently, considerable progress has been made in revealing the mechanisms through which plants sense and respond to high temperature, using *Arabidopsis thaliana* as a model system. When temperatures continue to increase, plants begin to experience heat shock stress. At this stage, plants can still grow, but apparent harmful effects begin to appear, mostly in reproductive development. These include the inhibition of male and female gametophyte development, inhibition of anther opening, inhibition of pollen germination and pollen tube growth, disturbances in pollen tube guidance and fertilization and abortion of early embryos (Hedhly 2011, Sage et al. 2015). Heat stress might concurrently affect membrane fluidity, causing the malfunction of chloroplasts and mitochondria, and denature proteins in the cytosol or endoplasmic reticulum, resulting in increased cytosolic calcium, reactive oxygen species (ROS) and nitric oxide (NO) levels and the activation of cytoplasmic protein response (CPR) and unfolded protein response (UPR). In some cases, temperature changes may influence a number of processes that control seed germination, including membrane permeability and the activity of membrane-bound and cytosolic enzymes (Gul and Weber 1999). It has been revealed that the alternating day and night temperatures encourage germination in a number of halophytes (Okusanya 1977).

The accumulation of ROS is another significant cellular response to HS in plants. Thus, ROS are then imported into the cell via aquaporins to regulate cellular thermoresponsive mechanisms (Bienert et al. 2007). There might be a link between ROS scavenging and plant tolerance to temperature stress, as ROS could play a key role in stress perception and protection, thereby mediating important signal transduction events [2].

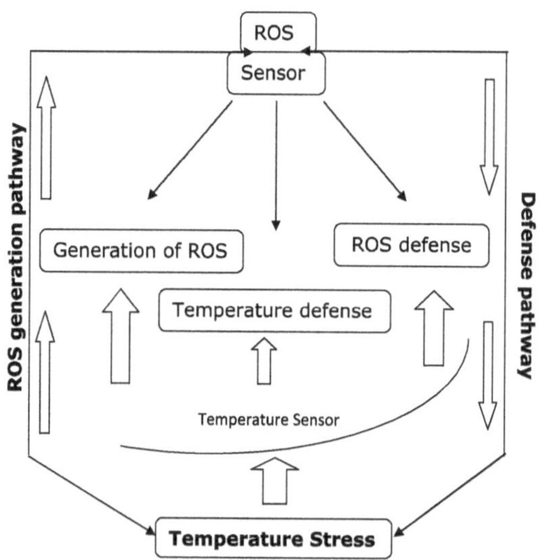

2. Role of ROS in temperature stress sensing and protection (Adapted from Suzuki and Mittler, 2006).

CHAPTER THREE

Response of Plants to Chemical Agents

Plants cannot stay safe. Desire for light spools grass out of the ground; desire for a visitor spools red ruffles out of twigs. Desire makes plants very brave, so they can find what they desire; and very tender, so they can feel what they find.

— Amy Leach, *"Things That Are"*

Every plant in natural conditions requires chemical resources for growth and developments, and they are able to establish these assets with the help of chemical receptors. Most of the natural interactions involved in plants are performed through different chemical reactions. Plants also both sense and interact through chemical reactions. These chemical receptors are available on cells of individual plants. There are two receptors ends located in the plasma membrane of plant cells, the outer end recognizes a particular chemical. The protein existing on the external part of the cell can bind to a chemical from the environment that can provide information about the existence of abiotic and biotic components or agents. The roots of some plants give off chemicals into the soil, making nutrients more available (Metlen et al., 2009). Darwin

(1875) postulated the existence of chemical signals in plants. Some plants also discharge chemical signals into the soil facilitating their inhabitation by mycorrhizae. However, in some cases, chemical agents such as H_2O_2, amino acid, ether, carbonic acid, $CuSo_4$ and ammonium sulphate are found to exert specific actions on growth. Their effect can occur –

a. by the strength of the solution

b. by the duration of the application and the condition of the tissue.

The above terms can modify their influence. Heavy metals such as copper, arsenic and cadmium in solution acts as toxic agents, retarding the rate of growth and ultimately killing the plants. The long-term action of the chemical exerts a stimulating activity, eventually leading to a depressing effect. Plant hormones, such as auxin and gibberellin, and mineral nutrients, such as nitrogen, are essential for the physiological and biochemical processes that occur in seeds and plants, and the responses from their metabolism are necessary throughout the plant life cycle, contributing to the linear increase in crop productivity. Activation of PAL activity is a typical response of plant cells to biotic and abiotic stresses and it may also function as an antioxidants because of its free-radical trapping properties (Haslam 1998). Nitric oxide (NO) is a uniquely volatile molecule in plants (Velikova et al. 2008). It is a signalling molecule that is implicated in the activation of plant defences. Nitric oxide is a bioactive free radical that plays essential roles in many physiological processes in plants, such as growth, development, senescence and adaptive responses to multiple stresses (Graziano and Lamattina 2005). Under ROS-related toxicity, NO may act as a chain breaker and thus limit oxidative damage. Recently, a function for nitric oxide has been reported in the protection of plants against oxidative stress under various adverse conditions (Shi et al. 2005). Many previous studies have reported the presence of NO in the plant kingdom and its involvement in growth, development and defence responses (Beligni and Lamattina 1999). Soluble sugars as important osmoregulation materials can decrease the osmotic potential and improve the stability of soluble protein. In addition to their storage functions, soluble sugars are considered to have an essential role in controlling cellular metabolism. Furthermore, plants or crops represent an outstanding source of bioactive compounds (Asif 2015), and pre-sowing seed treatment with chemicals weakens the plant tissues as well as the soil chemistry (Tzortzakis 2009). The application of chemical fungicides to manage plant pathogens, despite providing some relief, causes severe effects on the health of both humans and animals. Moreover, these fungicides provide worse consequences for the environment; they worsen the quality and productivity of the soil.

It has been suggested that under stress, soluble sugars can function in two ways, which are difficult to separate: as osmotic agents and as osmoprotectants (Bohnert et al. 1995). As osmoprotectors, sugars stabilize proteins and membranes, most likely substituting the water in the formation of hydrogen bonds with polar polypeptide residues and phospholipid phosphate groups (Strauss and Hauser 1986). The presence of amino acids, especially proline, may play a role in the protection from desiccation and the harmful effects derived from solute accumulation. Another most widely used strategy known as chemical priming refers to seed treatment with dissimilar chemical solutions used as priming agents. Such approaches includes priming with an extensive collection of natural and synthetic compounds such as antioxidants (ascorbic acid, glutathione, tocopherol, melatonin), hydrogen peroxide, sodium nitroprusside, urea, thiourea, mannose, selenium and chitosan, among others. The encouraging impact of chemical priming with a variety of priming agents in a wide range of environmental conditions has been indicated in numerous studies (Patade et al 2012). Studies have shown that seed priming with β-amino butyric acid increases drought or salt tolerance of green gram (Jisha and Puther 2015).

The application of ascorbic acid as a seed priming agent induces drought and salt resistance in wheat (Farooq et al. 2013). Several analyses carried out by Fercha et al. 2014 showed that priming with ascorbate neutralizes the negative effects of salinity stress via alterations in abundance of proteins involved in metabolism and storage. The most commonly employed chemical in osmo-priming treatment is PEG, generally due to its specific characteristic features. The large molecular size of PEG precludes its penetration into the seed thus avoiding the introduction of potential cytotoxic effects and diminution of osmotic potential within the seed (Di Girolamo et al. 2012).

However, proline can act as an osmoprotector of cytosolic enzymes and cellular structures (Csonka 1989). Proline accumulation may help the plant survive for short periods of drought and recover from stress. Additionally, the high proline concentration measured in sludge-treated nodules can also contribute a protective role as a scavenger of ROS (Koca et al. 2007). All of these factors can result in improved adaptation. Ascorbic acid (ASA) is the primary water-soluble antioxidant in plant leaves. As NO is now a commonly accepted second messenger in plants, it is supposed that a low concentration of NO might signal the inductione/stabilization of the expression of many antioxidative enzymes (Frank et al. 2000*)*. The protective effect of NO may also be related to its ability to react with some ROS such as O_2^-, making NO act as a chain breaker and revealing its proposed antioxidant properties (Conner and Grisham 1996). Moreover, it has been reported that NO can react with lipid alkoxyl ($LO^\cdot$) and peroxyl ($LOO^\cdot$) radicals, leading to the expectation that NO could halt the propagation of radical-mediated lipid oxidation in a linear manner (Lamotte et al. 2004). Thus, NO may help plants survive under stressful conditions through its action as a signalling molecule to activate antioxidative enzymes and direct reaction with active oxygen and lipid radicals. Additionally, the utilization of potassium nitrate (KNO_3) has long been recognized as an appropriate chemical method for enhancing germination in different plant species and usually as a priming agent or a medium for germination (McDonald 2000). It generates hormonal balance and diminishes the concentration of substances that slow down germination. However, the results of seed priming with KNO_3 on germination, seedling appearance and growth are well recognized.

CHAPTER FOUR

Electric Stimulus in Plants

Good fences make good neighbours.

– 17ᵗʰ Century proverb

The electrical experience in plants was first reported by L'Abbe Pierre Bertholon de Saint-Lazare and Scoot and Martin in 1783 and 1962 respectively. Plants use electrical signals to transmit information or signals within or between cells. The electrical stimulus helps to regulate many physiological functions in plants. It generates action potentials, induced in cell membranes where the electrical potential rises and falls, which also involves many cellular processes in plants (Beilby 2007). Other such examples of an electrical effect in higher plants have been widely studied and involve rapid associations (Umrath 1929) Such as the action potentials in the leaves of *Mimosa pudica* (Haberlandt 1890) and *Drosera intermedia* (Williams and Pickard 1972). Two types of electrical potentials are usually found in plants, namely, variation potentials and action potentials. The first is generated by wounding, cutting and burning, and it generally depends on xylem pressure and shows an effect on mechanosensory channels in adjacent living cells. The latter one, on the other hand, can be induced by mechanical, chemical or electrical stimuli or sometimes by cooling, exerting self-propagating signals that are transmitted at a constant velocity and amplitude

(Davies 2006). The study of electrical signalling in plants in a broader sense remains undecided, or detailed works are required. It may have apparent effects on physiological, photosynthetic, respiration and turgor regulations, among other responses of plant organs (Volkov 2006). In some plants, electrical signals are involved in the acuity of light, touch and temperature, among other. In fact, plants detect electrical signals with the help of glutamate-like receptors that also functionally mediate neural communication.

Additionally, tree planting can reduce electricity use and increase carbon sequestration. The impact of electricity on plant growth, development and accumulation of metabolites is not well understood to date. The effects of electricity, including active or weak electrical fields, magnetic fields and electric currents can have a visible effect on plant growth and development as well as on plant metabolites. The application of electricity is further considered to enhance plants in horticulture, and it is classified as an abiotic stress elicitor.

The term electricity is not sharply defined in the natural sciences, although specific properties belong to the core area of electricity. Electric fields, for example, are caused by electrical charges and can occur, e.g., under high-voltage lines (Feynman et al. 1964). Some positive effects of electricity on plant growth have been reported over the past 200 years (Tattar and Blanchard 1976). Lemström (1904) was the first to demonstrate the stimulating effects of natural electrostatic fields on plants grown under a Faraday cage. He also found that several plants exposed to high - voltage gradients (10 kV/m) from wires suspended above them were greener, sturdier and had on average a yield stimulation of 45%

compared with the control. A summary of different effects of electrical currents on plants and their membranes have been listed [**3**]. Other scientists have focused on the effects of pre-treating seeds with electrical fields on subsequent plant development. Zhang and Hashinaga (1997) exposed seeds of lettuce and radish to different intensities of alternating current (AC) and direct electrical current (DC) fields at a frequency of 60 Hz. These researchers found that AC electrica fields between 18 and 105 kV/m promoted germination of the examined plant species. These results were supported for AC by Moon and Chung (2000), who obtained an enhanced germination rate of tomato seeds in electrical field ranges from 4–12 kV/cm for exposure times ranging from 30–45s compared with untreated seeds. Additional studies have confirmed the interaction between electromagnetic, as well as electrical fields and the germination of wheat and barley (*Hordeum vulgare*) seeds (Lynikiene and Pozeliene 2003; Pittman and Ormrod 1970). Ward (1996) studied the influence of different DC intensities on hydroponically grown tomato plants, where the electrical contacts were placed at the top leaves of each plant and in the nutrient solution. He demonstrated that an electrical current flow of 125 µA. An applied downwards increased the shoot FW and shoot dry weight. However, an electrical current surge of 125 µA upwards led to improved uptake of calcium, potassium and magnesium compared with the control plants. Furthermore, Inaba et al. (1995) found that an externally applied DC at three mA for one hour promoted the biosynthesis of ethylene in cucumber (*Cucumis sativus*) fruit segments, which might have been a result of alterations in membrane function or plasma conditions. Recently, it was shown that a DC between 30 and 100 mA was sufficient to elicit the biosynthesis of secondary metabolites in intact roots in cell suspension cultures of a pea, fenugreek, barrel medic and chickpea (Kaimoyo et al. 2008). The researchers concluded that electricity elicited the biosynthesis of secondary metabolites in a broad range of plant species without adverse effects on the physiological functions of the cells or tissue (Kaimoyo et al. 2008). The exact mechanism of the electricity - induced changes in plant metabolic processes is currently not fully understood. Zimmermann et al. (1974) reported that free charges of opposite polarities exist on both sides of cell membranes, whereby a transmembrane potential occurs. As described above, Dannehl et al. (2012) suggested that weak electrical currents are responsible for the synthesis of more chlorophyll, which increases the absorption of light energy and photosynthetic activity. These plant responses may have led to higher generation of ROS and would explain the higher levels of phenolic compounds in garden cress required to protect plants against cell damage. A further gene expression study would be desirable to elucidate the molecular mechanisms of the change induced in plants by electrical currents.

Unfortunately, no other studies have discussed the possible signalling pathways affected by electricity to date (to the best of our knowledge). Therefore, the weak pulsed electrical field causes an accumulation of interior and exterior charges across the membrane, which can lead to a thinner layer due to the attraction between the opposite charges on both sides of the membrane. Thus, electricity can activate stress responses in both plants and seeds.

Species	Plant parts	Electric field conditions	Physio-biochemical effects	References
Triticum aestivum	Plant	40 kV/m	Increase in yields	[Blackman 1924]
Zea mays	seeds	10 kV/m	Increase in germination rate	[Florez et al. 2007]
Solanum lycopersicum	seeds	4–12 kV/cm	Increase in germination rate	[Moon and Chung 2000]
Lactuca sativa	Seeds	18–105 kV/m	Increase in germination rate	[Zhang and Hashinaga 1997]
Hordeum vulgare	Plant	10 kV/m	Increase in yields	[Lemström 1904]
Avena sativa	Plant	40 kV/m	Increase in yields	[Blackman 1924]
Cucumis sativus	Fruits	3 mA	Ethylene increase	[Inaba et al. 1995]
Zea mays	Seedlings	0.6 kV/cm	Increase in Phytosterol	[Guderjan et al. 2005]

3. Influence of electric field conditions on different plant species.

CHAPTER FIVE

Mechanosensing in Plants

Start with the leaves, the small twigs, and
the nests that have been shaken, ripped, or
broken off by the fall; these must be gathered
and attached once again to their respective
places.

– William Stanley Merwin, *"Unchopping A Tree"*

Plants usually recognize two different types of mechanical stimuli, static and dynamic. They react differently in a variety of ways. Most plant leaves and stems perceive positively, while some have a negative response. In addition, there are different mechanical perturbations of the shape of cells and other plant organs. For example, the downward growing roots tip perceives an obstruction such as stone. There are some other visible effects, as observed in models, in the behaviour of *Dionea muscipula* (hairs on the upper leaf surface become stimulated) and *Mimosa pudica* (rapid movement of leaflets and sliding movement of the entire compound leaf) among others. It is well-known that the sensitive plant responds to touch stimulation by the rapid folding up of the small leaflets composing the double compound leaves [4a, b]. The action potential is transmitted basipetally and successively stimulates the pulvinules to induce closure of the leaflets and it stimulates the sub-pulvinus to induce movement of the plant pinna. Various possible hypotheses concerning this mechanical signal perception mechanism show that mechanical stresses applied to cell-surface adhesion receptors (e.g., integrin-like proteins) can activate intercellular wounding signalling pathways, as in the case of animals or plants. These wound-activated responses (e.g., the production of secondary metabolites and senescence of local tissues) serve to cure the damaged area and activate defence mechanisms that prevent further damage in plants. The increase in action potentials, followed by a rise in reactive oxygen species (ROS) leading to the decline in elongation can also be observed in some plant species together with the induction and expression of touch (TCH) genes [5]. The mechanical stimuli that are induced by various environmental factors such as wind, touch, rainfall and obstacles may interfere with the growth and development of different plants (Puijalon et al 2011). The action of wind cause several types of mechanical damage, such as alterations in the cell wall (Houston et al. 2016), premature falling of leaves, breaking of branches and even uprooting of the entire plant, ultimately generating a series of physiological effects and changes in response to water loss, hormonal changes and reduced rate of cellular stretching, among others.

4. Morphological observation of *Mimosa pudica* L. (**a**) the compound leaves of *Mimosa* remain open before touch stimulation, and (**b**) the compound leaves goes folding up after touch stimulation. Image: **a**. Shaun Winterton, **b**. Juan Campa (Bugwood, CISEH).

It may also promote decreases in plant vitality, with consequent reductions of productivity (Langre 2008).

Some plant hormones, such as jasmonic acid have been found to function in conveying touch signals within plants (Volkov et al. 2010). Plants are usually capable of perceiving wounding signals from a large variety of probable invaders to broadly activated defence reactions under natural conditions. The response to mechanical injury is local or systemic, or both, thus engaging the generation, perception, and transduction of wound signals to initiate the expression of wound-inducible genes (Leon et al. 2001). In the initial stage, which likely occurs during appressorium formation prior to penetration of the plant cell wall, the perception of a local mechanical signal from the munching action is sufficient to encourage local cell responses such as the oxidative burst, cytoplasmic rearrangements and local cell wall thickening (Mayer et al. 1998). Early studies of mechanical stress have typically used simple physical contact with plant tissues to observe cell growth, callose deposition, and ethylene synthesis responses (Jaffe and Forbes 1993). Bending, abrasion, and influential factors are the main patterns of forces produced by experimental mechanical stressors applied to plants, since they are closely related to the loads encountered under naturally windy conditions. Numerous studies have demonstrated that these treatments of whole plants, or at the tissue or organ level, might reflect the evolution of species and growth of individuals, as well as the translocation of sub-cellular organelles and instruction of genetic expression. Sound waves, which are considered a mechanical stress, also have a noticeable effect on the growth and augmentation of plants or plant tissues in nature.

Responses to wind may vary between different parts of the plant. Leaves are the most intolerant organs to this type of stress, the effects of which directly alter photosynthesis and transpiration in plants (Huang et al. 2016, Schymanski and Or 2016). Additionally, depending on the leaf characteristics and wind speed, in some cases, a partial reduction or total elimination of the boundary air layer is noticeable on the leaf surface (Wada et al. 2014, Taiz and Zeiger 2013). Hence, partial reduction usually occurs in an environment of weak or moderate wind, consequently increasing gaseous exchange at the leaf level, and total elimination is generally established in the presence of strong wind, which also promotes stomatal closure. In some cases, increased transpiration reduces the leaf temperature and can also dehydrate plants (Onoda and Anten 2011). Therefore, the effects of wind can increase (Nagano et al 2009) or reduce the photosynthetic rate, reducing CO_2 diffusion resistance (Lambers et al. 1998) or lowering leaf temperature below the optimum level, and promoting stomatal closure, to avoid excessive water loss (Huang 2016, Schymanski and Or 2016). Notable macroscopic and microscopic mechanical injuries have been observed, which may result from constant leaf movement in the pulvinus and lamina of mature and young leaves, exposed to wind with different exposure times (during the first hour of exposure). Ultrastructural alterations are apparent, involving rupture of the cell membranes of the pulvinus and mesophyll tissues, followed by programmed cell death, mainly in the masses of young leaves. Despite this progress, there are no well-known mechanoresponsive receptors for plants (Monshausen and Gilroy 2009). Most recent reports link the involvement of the plant hormone jasmonic acid in response to touch (Chehab et al. 2012). Mechanosensing is an important environmental cues in plants. Some other mechanical stimuli that result in transient increases in Ca^{2+}, such as wounding, also induce a rise in Ca^{2+} in small or isolated groups of cells that are some distance from the wound, as well as at the wound site itself. Little is known about the signalling events and components that link the perception of mechanical signals to gene expression in plants. Ca^{2+} has been previously identified as being potentially involved. Hence, the mechanism by which a plant perceives mechanical stimuli or signalling in plants remains almost unsolved. These stimuli, working on membrane systems at cellular level, play an important role not only in thigmomorphogenesis but also in various responses to environmental factors, such as water, temperature and gravity. This property has led to the exploration of a mechano-sensor or a mechano-receptor at the membrane level that perceives these stimuli in plants. A thigmomorphogenetic influence on stem growth has been reported in many herbaceous and woody species (Biddington 1986). The mechanical encouragement imposed on young internodes of plants reduces their elongation and augments their radial expansion, and the experimental evidence obtained under natural conditions, such as wind, demonstrate that shaking or bending results in a decrease in elongation, but in some species also results in a promotion of radial growth. The application of weights to leaf petioles has also been performed to exert tensile stress on axial cells and verified transcriptional regulation of the expression of cell wall reinforcement proteins in stressed cells (Elliott and Shirsat 1998). Hence, to attain more insight into the underlying mechanisms, many experimental studies under more practical conditions have been conducted, using different kinds of mechanical loading systems. Additionally, mechanical stimulation induced by rubbing the internodes of plants has been shown to decelerate plant growth (Thonat et al. 1997). The difficulty in understanding the complex impacts of wind on plants is that wind acts not as a only stimulus but also has two quite different effects- it increases the air flow past the leaves, and automatically stimulates the plant, in particular by flexing the plant stem. The response to physical damage is frequently linked with primary biochemical processes, such as the creation of melanin-based pigments, leading to the blue-black staining of subdermal tissues. Researchers such as Johnson et al. (2003) imposed direct mechanical stress on potato tubers in order to explore the early cellular response and the rapid accumulation of superoxide radicals.

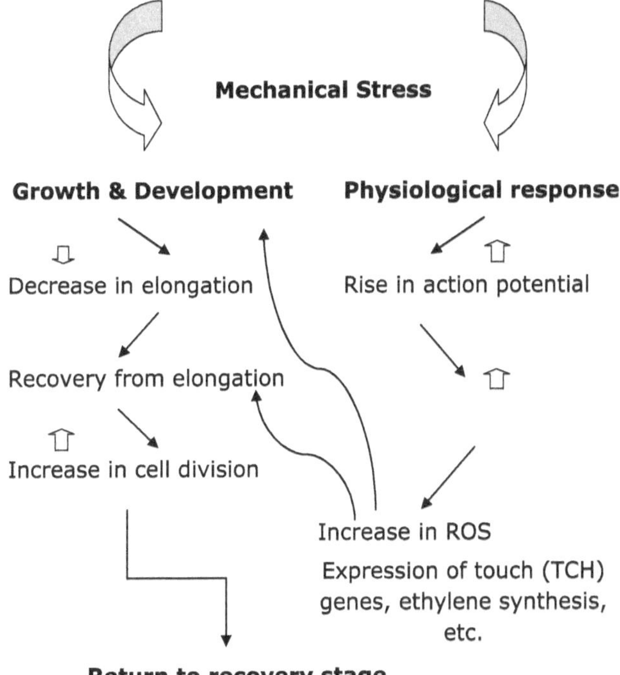

5. Responses of Mechanical stress and its recovery (Adapted from Telewski 2006).

CHAPTER SIX

Responses to Light

The velocity of light is one of the most
important of the fundamental constants of
Nature. Its measurement by Foucault and
Fizeau gave as the result a speed greater in
air than in water, thus deciding in favor of the
undulatory and against the corpuscular theory.
Again, the comparison of the electrostatic
and the electromagnetic units gives as an
experimental result a value remarkably
close to the velocity of light–a result which
justified Maxwell in concluding that light
is the propagation of an electromagnetic
disturbance. Finally, the principle of relativity
gives the velocity of light a still greater
importance, since one of its fundamental
postulates is the constancy of this velocity
under all possible conditions.

– A. A. Michelson, *Studies in Optics*

Plants require light to carry out photosynthesis and other critical physio-biochemical processes. There are four basic classes of photoreceptors in plants. The phytochromes absorb red (R) and far-red (FR) light and have a role in almost every phase of development, from germination to flowering to seed setting. Light serves as a significant regulatory environmental signal in the germination of desert plants (Baskin and Baskin 1995), since seeds may experience a transition from primary to secondary dormancy and then have a light requirement to activate germination. The requirement for light is a genetic trait and is mediated by phytochrome (Jones and Hall 1979), which encourages the amalgamation of growth-promoting substances to initiate germination in plants (Okusanya and Ungar 1983).

Light plays a crucial role in regulating plant growth and development through the modulation of theexpression levels of light-responsive genes that control developmental and metabolic processes. Plants use light energy as one of the substrates for carrying out the process of photosynthesis, which results in the O_2 that sustains life on this planet. When light energy exceeds the limit of what plants can use for photosynthesis, it results in the production of reactive oxygen species (ROS), which damage biomolecules, including the photosynthetic apparatus, causing light-induced photoinhibition. The excessive light excitation arriving at the PSII reaction centre can lead to its inactivation by direct injury to the D1 protein. Additionally, the excess accumulation of light energy by photosynthetic pigments also leads to excess electrons, outpacing the availability of $NADP^+$ to act as an electron sink at PSI. The excess electrons produced by PSI lead to the creation of ROS, notably superoxide (O_2^-). SOD and other ROS are low-molecular-weight molecules that are involved in signalling and, in excess, cause oxidative damage to proteins, lipids, RNA, and DNA. In natural environments, plants receive light energy from the sun. Sunlight, which we observe to be white, is actually composed of all possible colours of light. Light is frequently referred to as the most important resource for plant photosynthesis and growth in natural environments. Plants have two types of photoreceptors- photosynthetic pigments that gather light for photosynthesis, and photosensory receptors that regulate non-photosynthetic light responses. Light is important for photosynthetic plants, as it is the main source of energy for maintaining the physiological and biochemical functions of the plant, as a result, has a vast influence on plant maturity (Thomas 2006).

In plants, light signals are perceived by least four distinct families of photoreceptors - phytochromes (Phy), cryptochromes, phototropins and unidentified ultraviolet B photoreceptors. Each photoreceptor contributes to the perception of light signals for one developmental response, and signal integration indicates that the different light signals exist in various transcriptional hierarchies. Light signals can modulate photoreceptor activity by inducing changes that alter their cellular localisation. In plants, photosynthetic pigments absorb wavelengths (red) as leaves produce carbohydrates from CO_2 and H_2O. The photoreceptors sense light, enabling the plant during bud elongation and shoot initiation. The ratio of red to far-red light within the plant cells could regulates the expression of plant genes. Various reports have indicated that plant responses to light maximise their fitness in artificial environments and in natural conditions. The best characterised light receptor is Phytochrome, which exists in two photochemically interconvertible forms, Pr and Pfr, and is encoded by a small family of genes in angiosperms. The plant relies on three different types of receptors that distinguish light, phytochromes, cryptochromes and phototropin (Smith 2000). Leaves selectively take up red wavelengths and reflect green wavelengths; again red wavelengths are engaged by chlorophyll, as it produces carbohydrates from carbon dioxide and water. The responses of plants to light mechanisms are complex - seed germination, chloroplast development, photokinesis, pigment biosynthesis, flowering, senescence, etc. (in Kendrick and Kronenberg 1994). However, excess light can lead to a range of environmental conditions such as salt, toxicity, and temperature and can induce the augmented production of ROS, limiting the capacity of a plant to utilise light energy through photosynthetic mechanisms (Shinozaki and Yamaguchi-Shinozaki 2000). Excess light can lead to the inactivation of photosynthetic functions and the production of reactive oxygen species (ROS) such as hydrogen peroxide (H_2O_2), superoxide (O_2^-), hydroxyl radicals, and singlet oxygen in plants (Niyogi 1999). Elevated light decreases the redox potential of plastoquinone (PQ) regulating the expression of two cytosolic peroxidases during light stress (Karpinski et al. 1999). Plant responses to light are studied at different scales. At the subcellular level, the reaction can alter gene expression (Gilmartin et al 1990), but other possible associated actions are transient changes in membrane permeability (Pike 1976) and modulation of the activity of specific enzymes (Sibley and Anderson 1989). Light is a source of energy for photosynthesis and a source of information for photoperiodism (night/day length), phototropism (light direction), and photomorphogenesis (light quantity and quality). Light regulation is driven by different mechanisms in plants, but some are particularly important, such as the redox (Buchanan and Balmer 2005), photoreceptor-dependent, circadian clock (Dodd et al. 2005), and photoperiodic (Thomas and Vince-Pruce 1997) regulatory systems. Light is an essential contributing factor in the evolutionary selection of the chemicals used for photosynthesis (Blankenship and Hartman 1998). Green algae and higher plants utilise chlorophylls (a and b) and a variety of carotenoids to capture light for photosynthesis (Glazer 1980).

Plants possess two types of photoreceptors: photosynthetic pigments that harvest light for photosynthesis, and photosensory receptors that regulate non-photosynthetic light responses. Photomorphogenesis, i.e. the control of plant formation by ambient light conditions, is mediated by a set of photoreceptors. Photoreceptors are molecules that function at the interface between organisms and the environment. Plants rely heavily on these receptors, which absorb maximally in the blue (400-500 nm) and the red and far-red (600-800 nm) regions of the visible spectrum. Phytochromes are among the most critical environmental receptors/sensors in plants, and they regulate numerous aspects of plant growth and development from germination to floral induction (Chen et al. 2004). Nishio (2000) demonstrated the role of green light in carbon fixation within leaves and showed that green light drives carbon fixation deep within leaves. Both the palisade mesophyll (PM) and spongy mesophyll (SM) contribute significantly to carbon fixation (Nishio et al. 1993). Light absorption is mainly due to chlorophyll, whereas the pattern of fixation across the leaves is due to the distribution of Rubisco (Nishio et al. 1993). Chloroplasts are the primary photosynthetic apparatus of plants and their intracellular distribution depends on environmental factors, particularly the availability and quality of light. The opening and closing of stomata is vital for the gas-exchange processes that lead to photosynthesis and is affected by both light and hormones (Schroeder et al. 2001). In shade-loving plant, the morphogenesis, photosynthetic physiology and the growth of secondary metabolites of species, *Gynostemma pentaphyllum* are influenced by both light intensity and light quality or colour. The morphology and structure are directly affected by light energy. Plants involve various phototropic responses at the organ, cell and organelle levels in order to efficiently perceive light for photosynthesis. It is well established that plants respond to the direction of light (Briggs and Christie 2002). The bending of plant stems towards or away from a light stimulus is also arbitrated by blue light detected by the phototropic family of photoreceptors. Some plants can adjust their capacity for harvesting sunlight through their leaf and chloroplast movements. Increasing the intensity of the light causes plant growth to slow and eventually stop.

CHAPTER SEVEN

Influence of Magnetic Fields

There is a time and place for electromagnetic shielding and I regard it as a last resort due to the long term biological problems that I have observed with it over the years in plant growth experiments.

– Steven Magee,
"Curing Electromagnetic Hypersensitivity"

The influence of magnetic fields (both static and time-varying) on seeds and on plant growth and development is shaping into an exciting area of research. Recently, Maffei (2014) reviewed the events in this field, including the possible role of the geomagnetic field. The first study on the effect of a magnetic field on plants was conducted by Savostin (1930), who observed increases in the rate of elongation of seedlings, particularly wheat, under magnetic field conditions. The mechanisms by which plants are exposed to magnetic fields are not yet well known, but several theories have been proposed, including biochemical changes or altered enzyme activities, as proposed by Phirke et al. (1996). The positive effects of MF on seed germination have been reported by many researchers (Chen et al. 2011), and studies have suggested that the enhanced rate of seed germination and seedling vigour under the treatment of a magnetic field would influence the physio-biochemical processes that involve free radical formation and increase the activity of proteins and enzymes.

Krylov and Tarakonova (1960) proposed an auxin-like effect on germinating seeds from a static magnetic field and termed it magnetotropism. In terms of other types of radiation, gamma radiation increases the production of ROS in plants. However, plants have developed several enzymatic antioxidant mechanisms such as SOD, CAT and POX, to protect themselves from the damaging effects of ROS. Gamma radiation is also used to increase genetic variation in plants and to render them more productive and resistant. Some varieties of plants with commercial and agricultural significance have been developed using this type of radiation (Donini and Sonnino 1998). MFs are one of the natural components of the earth. Plants interact with magnetic fields in every day. Generally, the earth acts as a magnet with south and north poles, and the natural effects of magnetic fields affect plant growth and yield.

Increases in seedling growth, seed vigour and crop yield in seeds treated with static magnetic fields have been reported by Pietruszewski (1993). Several studies on the influence of magnetic fields on seeds and plants over many years have suggested that they lead to better plant growth and yield than chemical fertilisers and contribute to the improvement of crop productivity and protection. Additionally, magnetic technologies have been developed in several countries that are ecologically friendly, non-polluting to the soil and potentially attractive because they are affordable to farmers (Liboff et al. 1992). The treatment of seeds with magnetic fields (MFs) is a potentially safe and accessible physical treatment method that has been reported to significantly accelerate the release of seeds from dormancy (García-Reinaet al. 2001), and to improve seed germination and vigour (Alexander and Doijode 1995, Vincze et al. 2003), plant growth and vigour (Gubbels 1982) and plant yield (Wójcik 1995). Additionally, MFs induces an increase in seed water uptake (García-Reina et al. 2001), seed enzymatic activity and essential nutrient uptake into leaves (Esitken and Turan 2004), chlorophyll pigment content (Novitsky et al. 2001), and protection against heat stress (Ruzic and Jerman, 2002) and pathogens (Sadauskas et al. 1987, Pál 2005) without adversely affecting the environment. Likewise, extremely low frequency (ELF) MF exposure significantly changed the activity of several enzymes (alkaline phosphatase, protease, polyphenol oxidase, catalase, and nitrate reductase) and accelerated the synthesis of total protein in soybean seedlings (Radhakrishnan and Kumari 2012). The most prominent effects of magnetic fields on living systems, particularly their effects on seed germination and plant growth, have been the objects of numerous studies. Consequently, the magnetic treatment of seeds contributes to the enhancement of post-germination plant development and crop stands. Additionally, the biophysical mechanism behind the influence of MFs on plant physiological processes has still not been identified. As radical pairs are the only plant constituents that respond to external magnetic fields, a magnetic field is a precise tool for studying the importance of the reactions of photosynthetic radical pairs. External magnetic fields affect the results of radical pairs, including the first pair of PSII (see reviews by Hoff 1981, Rodgers and Hore 2009).

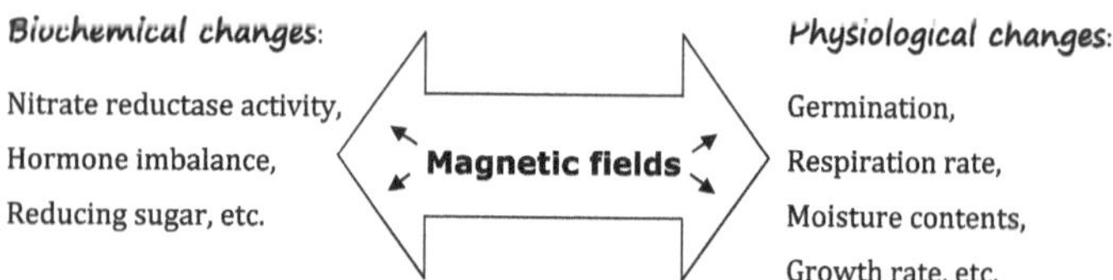

6. Possible physio-biochemical changes that occurs in plant under the influence of magnetic fields.

Specific physiological and biochemical changes occur in plants that may be due to magnetic influences in natural or artificial conditions [6]. In an external magnetic field, only the middle triplet energy level becomes populated during the short lifetime of a photosynthetic radical pair, and therefore, a magnetic field lowers the triplet yield of charge recombination in photosynthetic reaction centres (Hoff 1981). Thus, a magnetic field is also expected to reduce the amount of $^1O_2$ produced by the charge recombination mechanism. Here, the mitogen-activated protein kinase (MAPK) cascade is important and is one of the major pathways by which extracellular stimuli are transduced into intracellular responses in all eukaryotic cells (Wrzaczek and Hirt 2001). Most biotic and abiotic stresses, together with oxidative stresses, can activate defence responses in plants through the MAPK pathway. The activated MAPK can facilitate its translocation to the nucleus, where it can phosphorylate and turn on transcription factors, in order to modulate gene expression in plants (Melanie et al. 1995).

Nevertheless, magnetic field effects in plants seem to require stronger fields than those found in nature, suggesting that these phenomena are side effects of radical pair reactions (Katz et al. 1978, Rodgers and Hore 2009).

However, under natural magnetic influences, seeds sprout faster and develop deeper roots, and plants show higher growth rates and vigour, and are less susceptible to weeds and diseases. A visual comparison between the germination phases of blackgram (*Vigna mungo* L.) and soybean (*Glycine max* L.) seeds growing after exposure to MF is shown [7]. Under a magnetic field, the plants had a higher sugar content, oil content, and protein content when treated with south pole of the field. The south pole managed plants showed a more positive influence since the south pole of a magnet encourages energy and growth while, the north pole decreases the life activity of any plants.

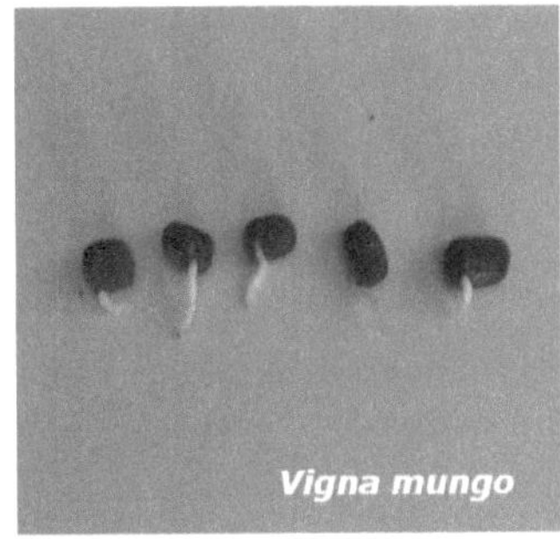

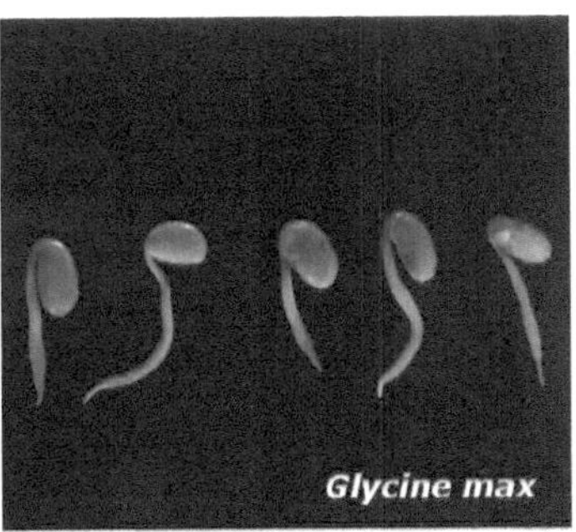

7. Visual comparison during germination phase of pulses seed after post exposure to MF.

CHAPTER EIGHT

Drought and Heat Adaptation in Plants

> One of the nice things about water plants is
> that they never need watering.
>
> – Christopher Lloyd,
> *"The Well-Tempered Garden"*

Drought and heat are critical environmental stresses or environmental changes that limit crop yield, severely affect agriculture and productivity. The air is not a good conductor of heat. High temperatures lead to high evaporation rates and water deficits. The resulting increased enzyme turnover leads to plant death. Efficient protein repair systems and general protein stability support plant survival and temperature acclimation. Heat stress also suppresses linear electron transport through photosystem II and instead stimulates cyclic electron transport around PSI (Sharkey 2005). At sufficiently high temperatures, the structure and function of the thylakoid membrane and photosynthetic proteins can also become damaged (Sharkey 2005). During heat stress, cellular respiration is affected much later than photosynthesis (Samuelson and Teskey 1991, Ryan 2011). Despite recent advances in our understanding of the mechanisms implicated in heat stress sensing in plants, many questions remain unanswered. The most important question may be, how are the different heat-sensing pathways incorporated? It is unknown whether the triggering of one pathway is necessary to initiate the others in natural environments. The inability to transport water to leaves leads to a decline in photosynthesis as well as leaf rolling and other morphological adaptations. Stoma closure reduces the evaporative transpiration induced by ABA. Plants, in response to rapid 5 to 10 °C increases in temperature, generate a unique set of chaperone proteins referred to as heat shock proteins (HSPs). Cells that have been triggered to generate HSPs show enhanced thermal tolerance and can tolerate exposure to temperatures that would otherwise be fatal. Plants act as an essential part of the ecosystem and may serve as a potential transport pathway for the uptake of carbon nanomaterials into the food chain.

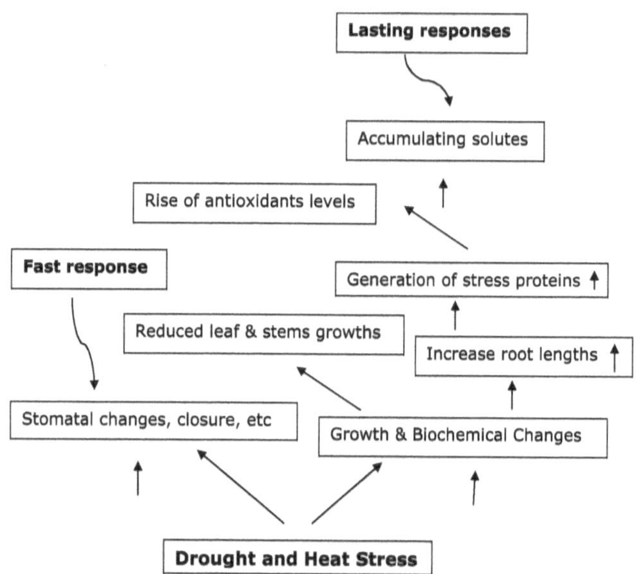

8. Plant responses to Drought and Heat stress.

It is vital to assess the interaction mechanisms between carbon nanomaterials and plants. More importantly, preliminary studies have shown that abscisic acid (ABA), one of the most critical stress hormones, plays a vital role in eliminating oxidative damage by improving the antioxidant system, such as superoxide dismutase (SOD), catalase (CAT), and the ascorbate (ASA)-reduced glutathione (GSH) cycle (Wei et al. 2015, Shan et al. 2017).

During warm seasons, the high temperatures limit photosynthesis and carbohydrate accumulation, increase cell membrane damage and cause protein folding and even cell death in C_3 plants. The same injuries have been reported in warm-season plants, such as C_4 plant species, during the winter. Additionally, the C_4 species absorbed less water and needed to modify themselves to be able to uptake nutrient elements with low solubility (Calatayud et al. 2008). In response to drought and adaptation plants have developed various mechanisms that increase desiccation tolerance and water retention. These responses have been divided into fast and long-lasting responses [**8**]. Heat stress delays flowering in *chrysanthemum*, a short-day plant. Heat stress-induced delayed flowering in this species correlates with reduced expression of *FLOWERING LOCUS T-like 3* (*FTL3*), an FT homologue (Nakano et al. 2013). The effects of heat stress depend not only on the exact temperature but also on the duration of heat stress and whether heat stress occurs gradually or suddenly (Yeh et al. 2012). Drought causes an early arrest of floral development and leads to sterility (Su et al. 2013). To ensure their survival during drought stress, plants often accelerate the flowering process, this response is known as 'drought escape' (Franks et al. 2007).

The related concept 'drought avoidance' refers to the condition where the plant reduces water loss to prevent dehydration (Kooyers 2015). Several characteristics have been shown to be relevant in drought stress tolerance, including early flowering and cropping, root deepness, the conservative pattern of water use and the induction of the production of enzymes (such as catalase, ascorbate peroxidase, etc.) that confer protection from reactive oxygen species and a pro-oxidative state (Foyer 2005, Poltronieri and Miwa 2015). Heat stress also delayed the emergence and expansion of new bud leaves by restricting the number and area of mesophyll cells. Increased heat stress leads to the overproduction and accumulation of various organic and inorganic osmolytes. These osmolytes protect the plants from stress through cellular osmotic adjustment, ROS detoxification, biological membrane protection and enzymes/proteins stabilisations (Bohnert and Jensen 1996, Verbruggen and Hermans 2008). Heat-sensitive plants lack this ability, and heat tolerance in such plants is improved by the exogenous application of such osmoprotectants and nutrients (Sakamoto and Murata 2002). Ongoing water deficit or drought leads to a disturbance in the association between membrane lipids and proteins as well as the enzyme activity and transport capacity of the lipid bilayer (Caldwell and Witman 1987). Drought is associated with enhanced heat tolerance in photosynthesis, i.e., the water deficit shifts the temperature threshold towards a higher value. The accumulation of metabolites consequently lowers the internal water potential and the resultant water attractiion at sub optimal temperatures limits plant growth and function. High temperatures restrict cool-season plant growth during summer in many regions of the world. The common visible morphological symptoms include leaf yellowing, rolling, leaf burns, etc. [9]. The optimum temperature for C3 plant growth has been reported at 15–25 °C by several scientists (DiPaola 1984).

9. Image showing burns and yellowing of leaves of *Brassica juncea* during natural drought stress in field conditions.

CHAPTER NINE

Flash-flooding or Submergence in Plants

One by one and then together the birds
chanted, warbled, whistled, and cooed, like
a rare desert plant bursting into life after the
rain.

– Mike Bond, *"The Last Savanna"*

Plant growth and cell development also depend on the supply of water, but water beyond the necessary amount or in excess leads to disturbances in the physiological, biochemical, ecological and molecular systems in plants. Every plant encounters these situations in their life cycle [10].

Most plants are unable to tolerate flooding or submergence for periods lasting longer than a few hours or days. These stresses may lead to anoxic conditions in the root system, leading to injury to the plant. Under critical oxygen stress, the mitochondrial respiration system that provides energy for growth in photosynthetically inactive roots will decrease and then cease, and the cells will start to die (Bray 2004). The results and effects of submergence or flooding generate anoxic or microaerobic conditions that interfere with mitochondrial respiration. Plant respond by developing cavities mostly in the roots help to facilitate the exchange of oxygen and ethylene between shoots and roots (aerenchyma). Submergence harms plants by limiting gas exchange and decreasing the incoming light. Among all of the abiotic stresses, flooding is one of the most significant environmental stress factors; it has a devastating effect on crop growth and ultimately causes reductions in yield and production (Normile 2008). Flooding strongly affects the productivity of farmland because most agriculturally vital crops are incapable of tolerating such stress (Setter and Waters 2003). SUB1, especially the Sub 1A gene, is an ethylene-response-factor-like gene that confers submergence tolerance on rice. It is expressed mainly due to declining rice sensitivity to ethylene, a plant hormone that encourages processes that cause plants to elongate and degrades their chlorophyll contents.

Flash-flooding is the saturation of soil with water. In waterlogged soil, the water table is very high, which affects normal biological activities (Jackson and Colmer 2005). Flooded conditions decrease root development, hence reducing the crop's ability to absorb water and nutrients and to tolerate drought stress during the season. Flooding is a significant strain in certain parts of the world, especially in rain-fed ecosystems, with poor drainage. Approximately 10 % of the global agricultural area is suffering from the constraints of flooding stress. Yield loss in various crops suffering from flooding varies between 15 % and 80 %, depending on the plant species, soil type, and time duration of the stress.

Nevertheless, lentil genotypes that are more resistant to flooding have been identified recently; these genotypes are characterised by large aerenchyma or air-spaces in their roots and by higher stomatal conductance compared to the more sensitive genotypes (Stoddard et al. 2006). The impaired ATP supply could be recognised as a primary cause of disruption to cellular homeostasis under other environmental conditions, such as flooding (Bailey-Serres and Chang 2005), with anoxia decreasing electron transport (lack of O_2 acceptors) and slowing ATP generation, such that cells become more reduced and the pH falls (Felle 2005). The anaerobic mitochondrial metabolism may have a more significant role than previously thought in alleviating the effects of anoxia on plant cells. Flash floods or submergence entail different plant stress conditions, that mainly depends on the water depth and the flood or submergence duration. Under complete submersion, concentrations of ethylene increase, which downregulates abscisic acid levels, and upregulates gibberellins levels. A typical plant hormone, gibberellins promotes the expression of genes that encode cyclins and expansins, which are associated with cell division and cell extension (respectively); this process leads to fast shoot elongation under water (Jackson 2008). Complete submergence is one of the most stressful scenarios that plants can experience in environments that are prone to soil flooding (Mommer and Visser 2005). In addition to root oxygen deficiency that occurrs during period of excess water in soils, plants subjected to complete submergence are prevented from obtaining enough oxygen to sustain tissue aeration, even though in some species, oxygen can partially be supplied by underwater photosynthesis (Vashist et al. 2011). As a result, the aerobic metabolism for energy production shifts to much less efficient anaerobic/fermentative pathways

(Kulichikhin et al. 2009). In addition, depending on the turbidity of the water, light reduction can constrain carbon gains through photosynthesis (Sand-Jensen 1989, Colmer and Pedersen 2008). Therefore, complete submergence can cause a drastic energy and carbohydrate crisis that can threaten plant survival (Bailey-Serres and Voesenek 2010). The adaptive traits of plants that enable survival under soil flooding and partial submergence are those directed to the oxygenation of submerged tissues (i.e., parts of shoots and entire root systems) and the presence of leaves above water to continue carbon fixation.

Plant under anaerobic condition

(FLOODING)

Only the upper or a portion of the shoot is covered by water

(PARTIAL SUBMERGENCE)

Only the upper or a portion of the shoot is covered by water

(COMPLETE SUBMERGENCE)

10. Representation of different stages of flooding or submer gence encountered by plants during their life cycle.

CHAPTER TEN

Heavy Metal Stress in Plants

In the course of centuries a huge and cohesive
network of interconnecting and partially
overlapping facts has been established which
we can call the scientific knowledge of nature.
It is, however, a net not without holes, and
some of the meshes are weaker than others.

— Erwin Chargaff, *"Serious Questions"*

Some soils have naturally elevated levels of heavy metals, and those plants that tolerate metal in soils are known as metallophytes. Plants respond to external stimuli, including heavy metal toxicity, *via* several mechanisms. These include (i) sensing of the external stress stimuli, (ii) signal transduction and transmitting signals to the cell, and (iii) triggering appropriate measures to counterbalance the adverse effects of stress stimuli by modulating the physiological, biochemical, and molecular status of the cell.

Non - protein thiols (NPT), glutathione, thiol-rich peptides (also known as phytochelatins) and other SH compounds (e.g., free cysteine), play an essential role in the detoxification of heavy metals in plants.

Heavy metal tolerant plants have critical potential uses as a mechanism to remove metals from soils (phytoextraction). The soils may either be contaminated with the metals through pollution by human activity (phytoremediation) or have naturally elevated metal levels (phytomining); in either case, the plant material can be harvested to remove the metal from the site. In either case, but particularly for phytomining, the harvested material can then be used to generate bioenergy, and the metals recovered can be used in the smelter stream or, if the recovery of the metal is not economically feasible, disposed of in a landfill.

The uptake of excess metal ions is toxic to most plants. The phytotoxicity of heavy metals can be attributed to the symplastic accumulation of heavy metals, particularly in the plasmatic compartments of the cells, such as the cytosol and the chloroplast stroma (Brune et al. 1995).

Metal-induced changes in development are the result of either a direct and immediate impairment of metabolism (Van Assche and Clijsters 1990) or of signalling processes that initiate adaptive or toxicity responses that need to be considered active processes in the organism (Jonak et al. 2004). The detoxification of heavy metals by plants is accomplished by uptake and translocation, sequestration into the vacuole and metabolization, including oxidation, reduction or hydrolysis and conjugation with glucose, glutamyl cysteine synthase (GSH) or amino acids (Dietz and Schnoor 2001).

The tolerance of plants to individual metals, although it forms the functional basis for the behaviour of "indicator" or "accumulator" plants, is often misunderstood.

Human-made alterations in the environment, such as those resulting from mining operations, result in similar selection pressures, as is evident from a cursory examination of these sites. HM toxicity has also become one of the critical factors responsible for limited plant growth under natural conditions (Upadhyay 2014). The term 'heavy metal' refers to any metallic element that has a relatively high density and is toxic or poisonous, even at low concentrations (Lenntech 2004).

HMs infect the environment by affecting soil properties, fertility, biomass and crop yields, and ultimately human health.

Heavy metals are a major environmental pollutant that originates from human activities, mostly as industrial wastes (Weisberg et al. 2003). Their accumulation in the soil is dangerous to all kinds of organisms, including plants (Gichner et al. 2006).

The induction of proline accumulation in response to abiotic stress may be due to an increase in its de novo synthesis or decreased degradation (Kasai et al. 1998) and the effect of proline on the permeability of the membrane (Pesci, Reggiani 1992). Therefore, the increase in proline could be measured as an indicator of tolerance to heavy metal stress.

Chlorophyll is essential for photosynthesis and is very sensitive to environmental stresses, such as heavy metals (Ekmekci et al. 2008).

A higher impact of heavy metals was observed on root growth compared to shoot growth, leading to a reduction in root length and fresh weight (Elloumi et al. 2007). The decrease in root length due to the accumulation of metals within the root reduces the rate of mitosis in the meristematic zones of roots, primarily by blocking metaphase in meristematic cells.

Heavy metals are essential nutrients in trace concentrations for healthy growth, as plants require these nutrients for crucial physiological functions (Tangahu et al. 2011). Deficient or toxic levels can cause disruptions to critical functions, leading to poor health or death (Nagajyoti et al. 2010) as well as to various morphological and physiological changes, as observed in the case of some aquatic model plants, such as *Pistia stratiotes* L. and *Spirodela polyrhiza* L. exposed to As and Cu [**11** and **12**]. For this reason, a novel technology known as Phytoremediation whereby metal accumulating plants remove, detoxify or stabilise pollutants at natural levels in contaminated sites can be applied for environmental remediation projects (for details, Salt et al. 1995). All plants, either in terrestrial or aquatic, have the capacity to accumulate metal ions such as Fe^{2+}, Mn^{2+}, Zn^{2+}, etc., which are essential for the growth and development of every plant. Some plants can also accumulate nonessential toxic metal ions. As a result, the perception has materialised that plants can be used to remove toxic metals from soil and water, thus contributing to the remediation of some polluted locations or sites (see Salt et al. 1999). Some aquatic plants have been explored for their potential to recover wastewater quality because of their capacity to grow or develop in water polluted by such heavy metals in the environment (see Reimer and Duthie 1993). Hence, plants have evolved a collection of mechanisms that control the uptake and accumulation of both essential and non-essential heavy metals. These mechanisms mostly include the chelation and sequestration of heavy metals by various ligands.

11. Images showing morphological changes in *Pistia stratiotes* L. under a - control, b - 10 µM, c - 50 µM and d - 100 µM concentrations of arsenic treatments.

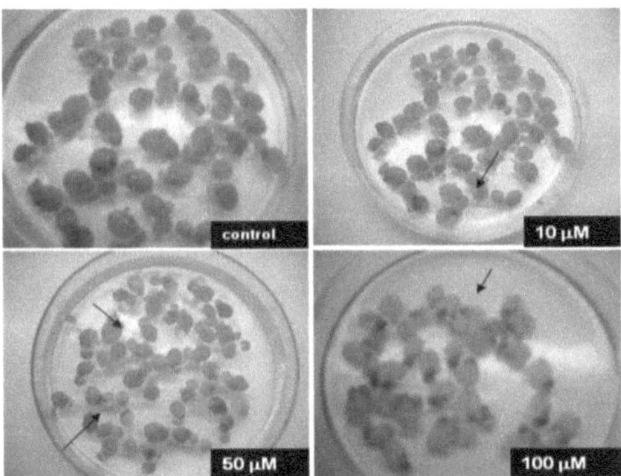

12. Images showing morphological changes in *Spirodela polyrhiza* L. under control, 10 µM, 50 µM and 100 µM concentrations of copper treatments.

CHAPTER ELEVEN

Pollution Effects and Plant Growth

There comes a time when the world gets quiet
and the only thing left is your own heart. So
you'd better learn the sound of it. Otherwise
you'll never understand what it's saying.

— Sarah Dessen, *"Just Listen"*

Environmental pollution is a global problem. It exists everywhere to different degrees and is specific to certain parts of the biosphere. The disposal of spent lubricating oil and other wastes used in cleansing during automobile servicing pollute the soil, once these waste materials enter the soil, they become part of the biological cycle that affects all forms of life (Mbah et al. 2009). Pollution caused by petroleum and its derivatives is the most prevalent problem in the environment (Millioli et al. 2009). These pollutants also have a directly toxic influence on plants when they contact plant tissues. However, plants respond to PHCs (petroleum hydrocarbons) differently (Sharonova and Breus 2012). Though industrialised countries control the release of toxic substances, in some developing countries, rapid industrial development and population explosions, together with a lack of requirements for pollution control, have caused substantial increases in the heavy metal contamination of natural and agricultural soils (Ji et al. 2000). The pollution in environments may also have a complex influence on mineral accumulation, as plant roots take in heavy metals from the soils and aerosols enter plants from the atmosphere through the surface of leaves.

The deposition of metal and the relocation of metals deposited on road surfaces by air and runoff water have led to soil contamination (Ogbonna and Okezie 2011). The effects of diesel exhaust emissions from vehicles on plant growth, flower development, leaf senescence and leaf surface wax characteristics have been studied (Honour et al. 2009).

Vehicles represent a significant source of air pollutants such as carbon monoxide (CO), nitrogen dioxide (NO_2), sulphur dioxide (SO_2), and particulate matter. Roadside vegetation, based on level road structures at 10 and 150 m from the road, could reduce NO_2 concentrations by up to 3.5 and 2.3 ppb, respectively (Nasrullah et al. 1994). In recent years, aquatic plants or duckweeds have become important because of their capacity to concentrate minerals from heavily polluted water from sewage treatment facilities.

Ascorbate is known as an antioxidant molecule that is able to detoxify air pollutants (Smirnoff 1996), and it is also able to control cell expansion and cell division (Conklin et al. 2000). Edible plants and vegetables are the main route through which arsenic enters food webs (Meharg 2002). Higher levels of arsenic in soil and water can influence the growth and development of plants, which may cause low yields (Farnese et al. 2014).

Some trees can remove a significant amount of pollution from the atmosphere as part of their standard functioning.

Green trees act as sinks and living filters to minimise air pollution through various processes such as absorption, adsorption, accumulation detoxification, etc., without undergoing foliar damage. Trees also improve air quality by releasing oxygen into the atmosphere. Particulate and gaseous pollutants are usually removed from the atmosphere by dry deposition and wet deposition. In dry deposition, pollutants are absorbed or adsorbed on plant surfaces. SO_2 could be incorporated into plant tissues through the stomata and react with water on inner-leaf cell walls to form sulphurous and sulphuric acids. These acids further react with other compounds and ultimately are transported to different parts of the plant. Some plants take up great quantities of pollutants and translocate them into vegetative organs at various rates (Kovács et al. 1993) which has a significant impact on the quality of the environment.

E-waste is hazardous because it contains toxic substances such as Pb, Cr_6, Hg, Cd and flame retardants (polybrominated biphenyls and polybrominated diphenyl ethers). E-waste mixed with solid municipal waste is posing a more significant threat to environmental degradation in developing countries. During combustion, other pollutants, including sulphur dioxide (SO_2) and volatile organic compounds (VOCs), are emitted together with carbonaceous particles from incompletely burned fuel droplets (Colvile et al. 2001). To create a defence mechanisms for their continued existence under conditions of high concentrations of diverse chemical elements, plants must experience natural selection either in polluted conditions or in an artificial selection program (Macnair 1993).

Soils on roadsides are the "recipients" of enormous amounts of heavy metals from a variety of sources, including vehicle emissions, coal-burning waste and other activities (Saeedi et al. 2009). Different water resources worldwide are being polluted daily through various anthropogenic activities. Arsenic is a commonly occurring toxic metalloid in natural ecosystems that enters ecosystems both naturally and through wastewater release from different industries. To prevent the hazards of toxic metal pollution, floating plants such as *Pistia stratiotes* L., *Eichornia crapsis* L., *Spirodela polyrhiza* L., etc. are biological components that have been successfully used in wastewater treatment. It seems very significant to expand and improve long-term passive monitoring techniques in order to understand the type and level of heavy metal pollution in any particular area.

Feng et al. (2011) suggested that heavy metals from traffic emissions may accumulate in roadside soils and plants. Meanwhile, other researchers reported that airborne heavy metals could be deposited and absorbed on the leaves (Nabulo et al. 2006). Plants such as mosses were developed as useful indicators at the end of the 1960s for biological monitoring of atmospheric depositions and heavy metal contamination in their environment (Ruhling and Tyler 1968). The use of native terrestrial mosses as biomonitors is now a well-recognised technique in studies of atmospheric contamination (Fernandez and Carballeira 2002) and is useful as a practical tool for identifying and characterising deposition sources. Another technique called phytoremediation is known to be economically cost-effective and helpful in environments that were damaged by mining activities, logging and industry. Phytoremediation is appropriate for any chemical pollutants in the environment. It also has important benefits to human beings and the surrounding ecosystems, such as reviving land and soil nutrient availability, and allowing the re-adaptation of vegetation to grow again in the area.

During the last decade, various biomonitoring studies using standardised indicator plants characterised the persistent phytotoxicity of air pollutants in those areas (Klumpp et al. 2002, Domingos et al.1998).

The cement industry has a significant role in the instability of the environment and produces many air pollution hazards (Stern 1976). Toxic compounds such as fluoride, magnesium, lead, zinc, copper, sulphuric acid and hydrochloric acid were found to be emitted by cement manufacturing factories (Iqbal and Shafig 2001). In recent studies, it was determined that cement dust pollution affected a variety of wild and aquatic plant species and their antioxidative enzyme systems (Erdal and Demirtas 2010, Mutlu et al. 2009).

CHAPTER TWELVE

Salts or Salinity in Plants

All organic beings have been formed on two
great laws- Unity of Type, and the Conditions
of Existence. By unity of type is meant that
fundamental agreement in structure, which
we see in organic beings of the same class, and
which is quite independent of their habits of
life.

...The expression of condition of existence...
is fully embraced by the principle of natural
selection [which] acts by either now adapting
the varying parts of each being to its organic
and inorganic conditions of life; or by having
adapted them in the long-past periods of time.

– Charles Darwin, *"On the Origin of Species"*

Salts the soils or water may inhibit plant growth for two reasons. First, the presence of salt in the soil solution reduces the ability of the plant to take up water, which leads to reductions in the growth rate of the plant. This phenomenon is referred to as the osmotic or water deficit effect of salinity. Second, if excessive amounts of salt enter the plant through transpiration, there will be an injury to cells in the transpiring leaves, which may cause further reductions in growth. This is called the salt- specific or excess- ion effect of salinity (Greenway and Munns 1980).

Plants in natural conditions absorb essential nutrients in the form of soluble salts, but the extreme accumulation of soluble salts, i.e., high soil salinity, holds back plant growth. Salinity is common in arid and semiarid regions. Salts in the soil occur as ions (electrically charged forms of atoms or compounds). The effects of salinity are threefold. Salinity reduces water potential and causes ion imbalances or disturbances in ion homeostasis and toxicity; this altered water status leads to the initial growth reduction and limitation on plant productivity. The detrimental effect is observed at the whole - plant level as the death of plants or as a decrease in productivity. Plants may vary in their responses to soil salinity under natural conditions. Salinity or salt-tolerant plants are better able to internally adjust to the osmotic effects of high salt concentrations than salt-sensitive plants. Salt-tolerant plants are more able to absorb water from saline soils. Salt-sensitive plants have a limited ability to adjust and are injured at relatively low salt concentrations. NaCl is a widespread salt, and the high concentration of ions, mainly sodium (Na^+), in the growing medium can produce cytoplasmic toxicity if taken up by the plant. Under salt-stress conditions, osmotic adjustment is frequently accomplished by the uptake of inorganic ions from the growth media. There are various factors that affect the ability of roots to extract soil water, including root morphology, water uptake rate, and root growth rate. Of all these factors, the least is known about root morphology and genetic variation in root morphology with genotype.

Salt tolerance is the ability of plants to grow and complete their life cycle on a substrate that contains high levels of soluble salt in natural and artificial conditions. Plants that can survive on high levels of salt in the rhizosphere and grow well are called halophytes. As soil salinization cannot always be corrected cost-effectively with conventional practices, the use of salt-tolerant rootstocks is the best solution.

Some are characterised by broader physiological diversity, which enables them to cope with saline and non-saline environmental conditions. Hence, an increasing interest in using omics tools, i.e., genomics, transcriptomics, proteomics, metabolomics, etc. to identify and understand salt tolerance components and mechanisms at the molecular level has been reported (Inan et al. 2004).

To engineer more salt-tolerant plants, it is essential to determine the critical components of the plant salt tolerance network. Recently, genomics, transcriptomics, proteomics, metabolomics, etc., have been successfully applied and provided exciting outcomes in unravelling the different components of salt tolerance in plants. These components include various genes (SOS signalling network), transcription factors (HLH, MYB, etc.), and proteins and metabolites (osmolytes, phytohormones, lipids, etc.) which may be used to engineer plants for increased salt tolerance. This multidisciplinary approach will be highly helpful in increasing plant as well as crop productivity to meet the increasing demand for food for the ever-increasing population.

Salinity or salt stress may lead to ionic stress, osmotic stress and secondary stresses, mainly oxidative stress, in plants. It also leads to elongation inhibition, yellowing, witling, etc., in the seedlings of some plants at early growth stages [13]. Hence, to adapt to salt stress, plants usually rely on signals and pathways that restore osmotic and reactive oxygen species (ROS) homeostasis in plants. During the past two and a half decades, genetic and biochemical analyses have revealed several core stress signalling pathways that participate in salt resistance. The salt overly sensitive (TSOS) signalling pathway plays a crucial role in maintaining ionic homeostasis, by extruding sodium ions into the apoplast. Another pathway, the mitogen-activated protein kinase cascades mediates ionic and ROS homeostasis. Some proteins are involved in maintaining osmotic homeostasis. Salinity affects more than approximately 5/6 % of the

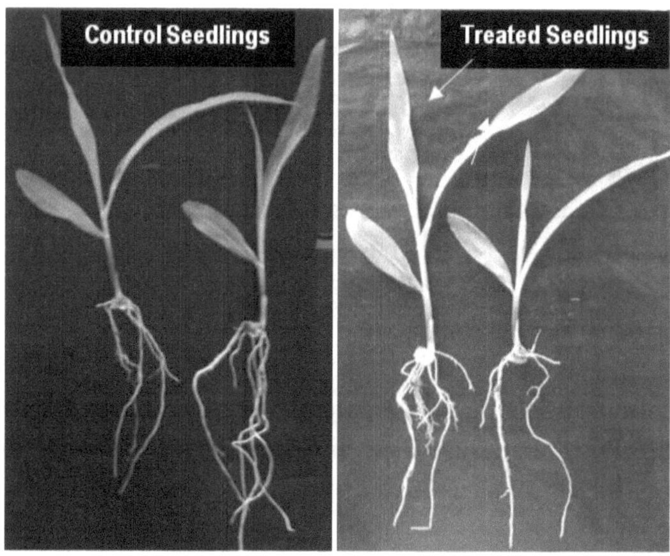

13. Photographs showing elongation inhibition, yellowing and changes in root and shoot growths of 13 d old Maize seedlings supplemented with 20 mM NaCl.

world's total land area (Munns and Tester 2008). It has increased due to poor irrigation practices, the improper application of fertilisers, and different types of emissions and industrial pollution (Ouhibi et al. 2014). Salinity is related to the production of reactive oxygen species (ROS) in plants. Several other redox sensors might also participate in the perception of disturbed ROS homeostasis to maintain redox balance control. Heat stress transcription factors (HSFs) might function as ROS-dependent redox sensors. As salt stress induces the accumulation of ROS, it generates oxidative stress-induced toxic effects in plants under stress conditions. In addition to their toxic effects, ROS also function as signalling molecules in response to environmental stimuli. These signalling molecules must be present at suitable levels in plant cells. Sometimes, human activities also result in soil salinization. Inappropriate water management practices related to intensive agriculture can cause substantial salinization of crop lands. Evaporation and transpiration remove pure water (as water vapor) from the soil, concentrating the salts in the soil solution. Soil salinity is also increased when water droplets from the ocean flow over land and evaporate. Detoxification signalling pathways are involved in controlling homeostasis during cellular ROS level formation under various stress conditions. Hence, the chance for stress injury is reduced once cellular homeostasis is re-established. Although several putative osmotic and redox sensors exist in plants, the identities of specific salt-induced stress response sensors remain unclear. Revealing these salt-stress sensors or receptors has become the most critical and essential goal in the field of salt stress signal transduction in plants. Hence, identifying these specific salt-stress sensors/receptors and their underlying mechanisms remains an exciting challenge in this area. Natural salinity or human-induced salinity results from the accumulation of salts over long periods through natural processes in the soil or groundwater. Under these conditions, ionic signalling for the restoration of cellular homeostasis under stress conditions, detoxification signalling to control and repair stress damage, and signalling to coordinate cell repair and cell expansion occur in response to the particular stress conditions [14]. Human-induced salinity involves salinization resulting from human activities such as land clearing and the replacement of perennial vegetation with annual crops or irrigation schemes using salt-rich irrigation water or having insufficient drainage. Salts can be decreased or removed from the soil by leaching if drainage is not restricted. Watering plants more often can reduce salt injury. The unfavourable effects of soil salinity can also be avoided by promoting vigorous growth through good management and adequate fertility. It is also believe that by comparing different genotypes and genetic combinations, researchers will be able to advance the field more quickly and develop salt-tolerant germplasms.

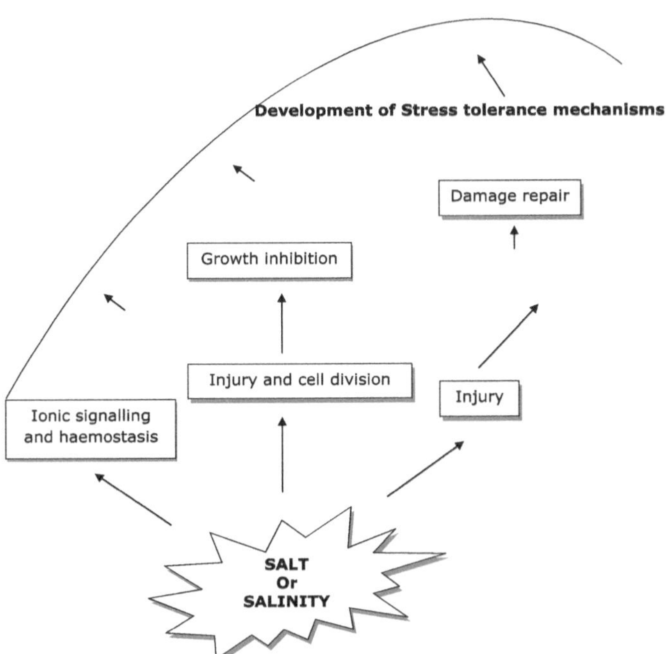

14. An overview of functional aspects of salt or salinity stress signalling pathways in plants.

CHAPTER THIRTEEN

Plant Adaptation to Biotic Components

What we are doing to the forests of the world is but a mirror reflection of what we are doing to ourselves and to one another.

– Chris Maser, *"Forest Primeval: The Natural History of an Ancient Forest"*

In natural environments, plants come in contact with different herbivores and microbes. They are always under attack by pathogens, pests, and parasites, resulting in severe consequences for global food production and human health. Plants experience these attacks through changes in the potential of the plasma membrane that surrounds the cell. These defence mechanisms allow plants to maintain their internal balance despite attacks from herbivores and pathogens. While pathogens and pests find ways to invade and communicate with their hosts, plants have evolved sophisticated immune systems to fight infections. In some cases, tobacco plants infested with TMV emit volatile methyl salicylate that coordinates systemic resistance in plants (Park et al. 2007). In the field of plant-microbial interactions, most studies have focused on the functional and signalling pathways of plant disease resistance (R) proteins and pattern recognition receptors (PRRs), as well as pathogen effector proteins. Plants, like all other organisms, are constantly challenged by microbial pathogens. Their static nature and lack of an active circulatory and immune system pose added disadvantages when dealing with such stresses. Thus, plants have developed some unique mechanisms to defend themselves from biotic stresses. Because of its essential role in plant immunity, the plant actin cytoskeleton is often targeted by various bacterial, fungal, and viral pathogens. In addition to proteins and RNAs, volatile organic compounds emitted by plants also serve as necessary signals for communication between plants and interacting insects and pests.

Bacterial pathogens often form biofilms, complex three dimensional bacterial assemblages, in different plant tissues or outside the hosts as an adaptive strategy to cope with host immune responses or harsh environmental conditions. A similar result was also reported by Castiblanco and Sundin (2016) who reported that bacteria produce 20–500 nt small noncoding regulatory RNAs, that also contribute to biofilm formation. Niu et al. (2016) described a growth-promoting rhizobacterium that primes induced systemic resistance by suppressing host R gene-targeting microRNA pairs and activating host immune responses. This finding further supports the critical role of endogenous small RNAs in plant-pathogen interactions. Large quantities of chemical fertilisers are used to replenish soil N and P, resulting in high costs and severe environmental contamination. N_2-fixing and P-solubilising bacteria are necessary for plant nutrition because they increase N and P uptake by the plants and play a significant role as plant growth-promoting rhizobacteria (PGPR) in bio-fertilisation. Enhancing and extending the role of bio-fertilisers could reduce the need for chemical fertilisers and decrease adverse environmental effects. There are several microorganisms that can also solubilise the less-expensive sources of phosphorus, such as rock phosphate. Bacteria such as *Bacillus* are widely used in plant production systems and are essential phosphorus-solubilising microorganisms; their application results in the improved growth and yield of crops (Dobereiner 1997). Some PGPR strains are known to have the potential to mitigate the effects of heavy metal contamination in the soil, as they reduce the toxic effects of heavy metals on plants by accumulating them (Belimov et al. 2004). In nature, plants also have to cope with insects and pathogens in order to survive. Most plants have developed some pathogen resistance through gene recognition, which is a compromise in which a plant can allow some "munching" but avoid virulent infestations. It is believed that attempted penetration by the pathogen generates not only chemical but also mechanical signals, and this combination of signals has to be clear to the plant in order for the plant to display its full complement of defence reactions (Mayer et al. 1998).

Soil microbes such as AM fungi and PGPR can alleviate the stress of heavy metals by absorbing high rates of heavy metals in their tissues. There are different mechanisms by which soil microbes can mitigate the unfavourable effects of heavy metals in their tissue, including intra- and extracellular mechanisms. Plants are exposed to a vast range of pathogens and pests. In natural ecosystems, the coevolution of genetically diverse plant and pathogen populations over millions of years has resulted in disease being relatively rare and geographically restricted. In contrast, agricultural environments with monoculture cropping systems often provide an environment for the selection of virulent pathogen strains, which can result in considerable preharvest crop losses, threatening food security (Boyd et al. 2012, Dangl et al. 2013). In addition to preformed physical barriers such as the cuticle and cell wall and the production of antimicrobial metabolites, plants also utilise induced defence-signalling mechanisms against microbes (Jones and Dangl 2006). These include nonhost resistance, pathogen-associated molecular pattern (PAMP) - triggered immunity (PTI), and effector-triggered immunity (ETI). In PTI, general pathogen elicitors are recognised by extracellular pattern-recognition receptors in the plant (Thordal-Christensen 2003). Conti et al. (2017) examined the effects of tobacco mosaic virus-encoded proteins on host plant physiology, focusing on replicase, a movement protein (MP) and a coat protein (CP). They discussed the effects of each viral component on the modulation of host defence responses through mechanisms involving hormonal imbalances, innate immunity modulation and antiviral RNA silencing. The individual and combined effects of viral-encoded proteins contributed to viral replication and movement in the host plant. Several biotic stress-induced factors, such as salicylic acid, nitric oxide hydrogen peroxide, or other unknown agents, promote defence gene expression and programmed cell death by inhibiting the function of the cytochrome pathway and electron transport chain components [15]. This dysfunction upholds increased reactive oxygen species

(ROS) generation by the ETC, thus initiating further damage and dysfunction in a self-amplifying manner and ultimately leading to the catastrophic dysfunction linked with permeability transition and loss of outer membrane integrity.

Induced resistance in plants is characterised by a latent defence response that, following induction, is activated only at a later moment, upon attack by a pathogen or an insect herbivore (Pieterse et al. 2012). This induced state of resistance is expressed systemically at the whole-plant level, not only in the plant tissues exposed to the inducer (Durrant and Dong 2004). Upadhyay (2011) found that rhizobacteria ameliorate the toxic effects of heavy metals by changing their valencies and bioavailability. Dary et al. (2010) demonstrated that the application of *Bradyrhizobium* sp., *Pseudomonas* sp., and *Ochrobactrum cytisi* alone as well as together decreased Pb in soil and the roots and shoots of *Lupinus luteus* after a mine spill. Indole-3-acetic acid (IAA) produced by microbes greatly interferes with the physiological processes of plants, and its level changes significantly during stress.

The growth and development of plants in response to environmental stresses involve multiple regulatory processes. Many studies have highlighted the effectiveness of rhizobacteria and their role in the bioremediation of PHC (Wang et al. 2016). During rhizoremediation, exudates derived from the plant can help stimulate the survival and action of bacteria, which subsequently results in the more efficient degradation of pollutants.

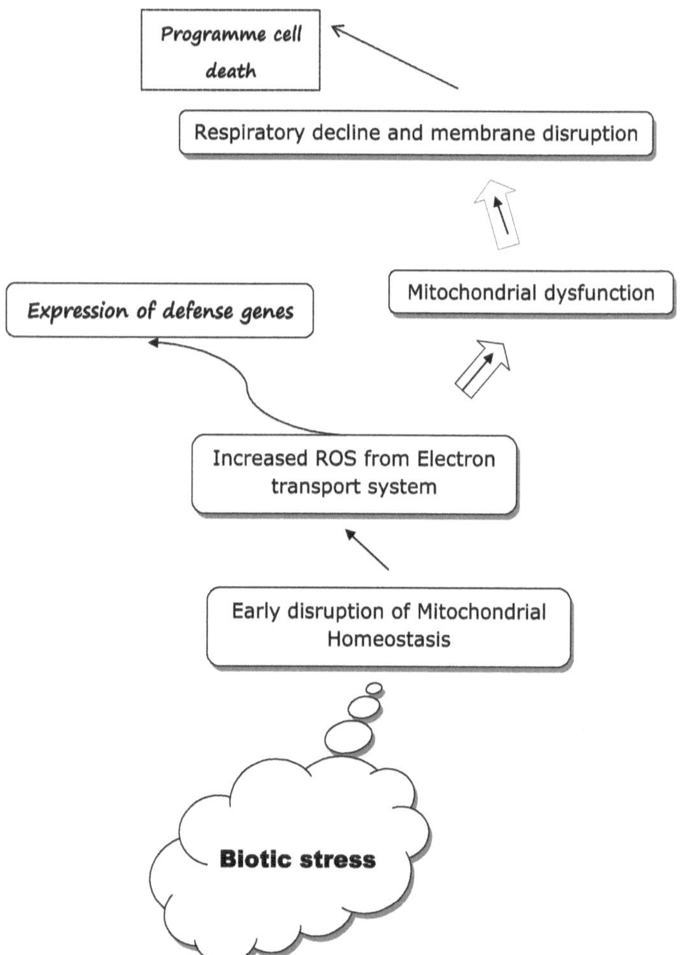

15. Role of mitochondria in plant responses to biotic stress.

Rhizoremediation is the application of bacteria that can survive in the root exudates of plants and contribute to sequestering, detoxifying, or degrading pollutants (Kuiper et al. 2004). Rhizobacteria not only mitigate heavy metal toxicity but also act as plant growth promoter (PGPs) for the crop. The rhizoremediation process has been reported to be a practical, low-cost, and socially acceptable technology for remediating polluted soils (Chibuike and Obiora 2014). A summary focusing on plant interactions or virus–plant interactions and their biotic factor responses in plants is provided [16]. Meeting the demands for food in the context of the current rapid global population increase is a significant challenge for sustainable agriculture, with global losses across crop species due to preharvest diseases currently estimated at approxmately 15 %. While plants and their pathogens are continuously coevolving, the continuous planting of cultivars in monoculture can favour the emergence of virulent pathogen populations that can overcome disease resistance. Similarly, many plant genes are regulated by biotic factors (e.g., bacterial pathogens, viruses, fungi, insects, nematodes, etc.) (Fagard et al. 2007). All these factors potentially affect the different levels of gene expression, including transcription, RNA processing, translation or even post-translational modifications in plants.

Species	Biotic stress factor	Biotic stress factor response	References
Brassica Juncia (Indian Mustard)	*Pieris rapae* (caterpillar)	Lethal	[Hanson et al. 2003]
Senecio coronatus	*Helix aspersa* (snail)	Toxicity	[Boyd et al. 2002]
Thlaspi caerulescens	*Pieris brassicae* (caterpillar)	Feeding Deterrent	[Pollard and Baker 1997]
	Deroceras carvanae (slug)	Feeding deterrent	[Pollard and Baker 1997]
Thlaspi goesingense	*Erysiphe cruciferarum* (fungus)	Virulent	[Freeman et al. 2005]
Arabidopsis halleri	*Helix aspersa* (snail)	No effect	[Hultson and Macnair 2003]
Nicotiana tabacum (tobacco)	*Turnip vein clearing virus* (TVCV)	Decreased virulence (blocks systemic spread)	[Ghoshroy et al. 1998]
Lycopersicum esculentum (tomato)	*Cucumber mosaic virus* (CMV)	Favors infection	[Miteva et al. 2005]
Triticum aestivum (wheat)	*Fusarium oxysporum* (fungus)	Decreased virulence	[Franceschi et al. 2005]

16. Responses of biotic stress factors on plant – pathogen interactions in different plant species (Adapted from Poschenrieder et al. 2006).

Agricultural practices can also facilitate pathogen movement to new areas, exacerbated by human migration and the movement of contaminated germplasm. The global tendency toward a reduction in dependency on pesticides for disease control means that the development and deployment of pest- and disease-resistant crop cultivars will probably play an increasingly important role in the intensification of sustainable agriculture. Climate change and the associated temperature increases have also been shown to increase the geographic distribution and reproductive potential of pathogens. Much ongoing research on individual stresses in plants is providing evidence for overlaps in receptors, signalling pathways and responses, not only between different biotic stresses but also between biotic and abiotic stresses. The synthesis of IAA by rhizosphere bacteria in metalliferous environments seems to be a plant defence strategy that is vital for plant growth and development (Mesa et al. 2015). Plants have naturally developed a variety of mechanisms for coping with stress conditions, including shifts in the physiology of the plant as well as the expression of stress - associated genes, which leads to the production of an extensive variety of low molecular-weight metabolites such as mannitol, proline, glycine betaine and polyamines (Rajam et al. 1998). Others substances such as polyamines (PAs), putrescine (Put), spermidine (Spd) and spermine (Spm) also play crucial roles in plant responses or defences against biotic stresses or environmental changes. These are tiny polycationic compounds that are present in all living organisms. In addition to their involvement in stress reactions (Bouchereau et al. 1999, Walters 2003), they also have a significant role in the regulation of a variety of cellular and molecular processes, including growth and development, membrane integrity and macromolecular synthesis and function (see Thomas and Thomas 2001). Weeds, on the other hand, are the most important biotic constraints to the implementation of a direct-seeded rice crop, as there is no standing water or seedling size advantage to hold back weeds at the time of crop establishment. Several biotic environmental factors, that result from interactions with other organisms, are, for example, infection or mechanical damage from herbivory, as well as the effects of symbiosis or parasitism. Generally, many studies on the effects of biotic stresses or changes on the action of antioxidant enzymes in herbaceous plants have been carried out, while studies on woody plants are less common. In addition, most of these studies have been carried out with leaf tissues, but those using seed tissues are limited. Among the biotic factors contributing to low chickpea production, collar rot disease, caused by *Sclerotium rolfsii*, is a major reason for the 50–95 % mortality of chickpea seedlings under natural field conditions. Currently, there are no substantial levels of host plant resistance for *collar rot in chickpea* though the disease that can be reduced through the use of fungicides and suitable crop rotation techniques. Some plants react to attack from pathogens by activating a variety of defence mechanisms, including phytoalexins synthesis and hypersensitive cell death, which limits the growth of pathogens at the site of infection (Kadota et al. 2004). These responses are preceded by the interaction between the pathogen associated molecules (elicitors) and the putative plant receptors (Vera-Estrella et al. 1994).

CHAPTER FOURTEEN

Waterlogging and Plant adaptations

By blending water and minerals from below with sunlight and CO_2 from above, green plants link the earth to the sky. We tend to believe that plants grow out of the soil, but in fact most of their substance comes from the air. The bulk of the cellulose and the other organic compounds produced through photosynthesis consist of heavy carbon and oxygen atoms, which plants take directly from the air in the form of CO_2. Thus the weight of a wooden log comes almost entirely from the air. When we burn a log in a fireplace, oxygen and carbon combine once more into CO_2, and in the light and heat of the fire we recover part of the solar energy that went into making the wood.

– Fritjof Capra, *"The Web of Life: A New Scientific Understanding of Living Systems"*

Waterlogging is the presence of excess water in the soil such that there is insufficient oxygen in the pore space for plant roots to be able to adequately respire. Excess rainfall can lead to the waterlogging of soils, the duration of which varies greatly depending on the amount of rain and evapotranspiration and soil structure. Waterlogging affects plant growth and yield in rainfed areas around the world. The main effect of waterlogging in plants is oxygen deprivation, which affects nutrient and water uptake, leading the plants to wilt even when surrounded by excess water. This phenomenon causes anoxia due to low oxygen levels, shifting the energy metabolism of plants from aerobic to anaerobic conditions. Plants differ in their demand for O_2. There is no level of soil O_2 that can result in waterlogged conditions for all plants. In addition, a plant's demand for O_2 in its root zone will vary with the growth stage of the plants. Waterlogging usually occurs in irrigated and high - rainfall environments. Due to the lack of proper drainage systems acts on the subcontinent, the Nile river, etc., and the excessive application of water to plants, the other crops tend to be overirrigated. Thus, the soils associated with plants and crops soils are slit or loam, which cause waterlogging by restricting percolation from the surface.

The lack of O_2 in different zones causes plants root tissues to decompose. Plant transpiration is affected until the roots recover or adapt to the anaerobic conditions. However, extended waterlogging will result in root death. Once a waterlogging event has passed, plants recommence respiration as long as soil conditions are moist; the relatively old roots close to the surface allow the plants to survive. However, further waterlogging-induced root pruning and dry conditions may weaken the plants to the extent that they will be very poorly productive and may eventually die. Many farmers do not realize that a site is waterlogged until water appears on the soil surface. However by this stage, plant roots may already be damaged and the yield potential may be severely affected.

Waterlogging during sowing or germination generally kills the seed or seedlings. The seedling radicals and roots do not adapt readily adapt to waterlogging. Generally, plant tolerance to waterlogging increases as plants age. Crops such as wheat can make an amazing recovery following early waterlogging stress if supplied with extra nitrogen. Waterlogging occurs when the soil profile or the root zone of a plant becomes saturated. This happens when more rainfall occurs than the soil can absorb or the atmosphere can evaporate.

Due to the changes in the texture of the soil as a result of waterlogging, productivity also decreases, thus causing a decrease in grain or crop yield and production. It also increases acidity build up which is harmful to most food crops. When the soil structure is affected and the cultivation of wet soil takes place, bacteria tend to reduce normal biotic activity, which affects root development. Waterlogged soil is slow to warm up. Low soil temperatures restrict root development and depress biotic activity in the soil resulting in a lowered rate of production in terms of the available nitrogen and hampering seed germination and seedling growth. This occurs because of the competition for nitrogen by the soil microorganisms that thrive in saturated soil and the reduction in the numbers of nitrifying organisms due to a lack of aeration. The severity of the effects of waterlogging depends on the growth stage of the plant. The non-structural carbohydrate concentrations in leaves and roots increase (Barrett-Lennard et al 1988). However, short-term and long-term waterlogging may also harshly change the growth and survival of the seminal root system in plants, thereby affecting the balance between root and shoot growth.

There is a reduction in nitrogen in the soil which affects plant nutrient uptake. The normal cultivation operations of tillage and ploughing are adversely affected due to the presence of excess water in the soil, which causes physiological disease to crops and the decay of roots, and external symptoms on the foliage and fruits are common. The maturity period of crops is reduced resulting in low yield. The yield of crops is adversely affected if the water is 90 cm in depth in the case of crops such as sugarcane (*Saccharum officinarum*) and 60 cm and 90 - 125 cm in depth in the case of wheat (*Triticum aestivum*). Waterlogged wild plants grow widely and compete with crops, thereby affecting the growth of useful crops and weed removal and entailing extra investment. Drainage can be improved on many sites and is the first thing to consider once a waterlogging problem has been identified. The proper installation and maintenance of surface drainage systems, including the use of raised beds, is critical for minimizing off-site impacts, especially where sediments and nutrients may enter waterways and threaten water quality - surface drainage starting with parameters, subsurface drainage, and raised beds to reduce soil compaction and improve the soil structure, etc. Improving the water holding capacity of the soil will reduce the probablity of waterlogging, increasing soil organic matter levels, reducing tillage and increasing the amount of surface cover to reduce the amount of soil surface sealing, among other benefits. This also assists in the reduction of water loss through evaporation. The application of nitrogen fertilizers after waterlogging has been shown to reduce the detrimental effects of stress. Waterlogging under optimum soil nutrient and nitrogen supply conditions resulted in less growth restriction than that under a suboptimal nutrient supply. The use of manures increased the availability of Fe and Mn several fold under flooded conditions. It can also improve soil physical factors and reduce soil surface crusting, enhance plant rooting and elevate the effects on yields. Moreover, those plants that are adapted to such conditions have certain mechanisms to deal with this stress such as developing aerenchyma, increasing the availability of soluble sugars, and introducing greater activity of the glycolytic pathway and fermentation enzymes and the involvement of antioxidant defence mechanisms to cope with the effects of hypoxia or anoxia or recovery after such stress. Sometimes, the gaseous plant hormones such as ethylene play an important role in adjusting the plant response to oxygen deficiency during waterlogging. In certain studies, waterlogging has been reported to induce the expression of genes of enzymes associated with aerenchyma formation, glycolysis and fermentation pathways. In addition, nonsymbiotic- haemoglobins and nitric oxide have also been recommended as alternatives to fermentation for maintaining low redox potential (low NADH/NAD ratio) and in that way play an important role in waterlogging tolerance and signalling. Hence, the characteristics that contribute to better growth under waterlogged conditions and rapid recovery include the slightest diminution of photosynthetic rate and chlorophyll contents and slow nutrient uptake, etc., until the plant is able to develop detoxification systems after waterlogging [**17**].

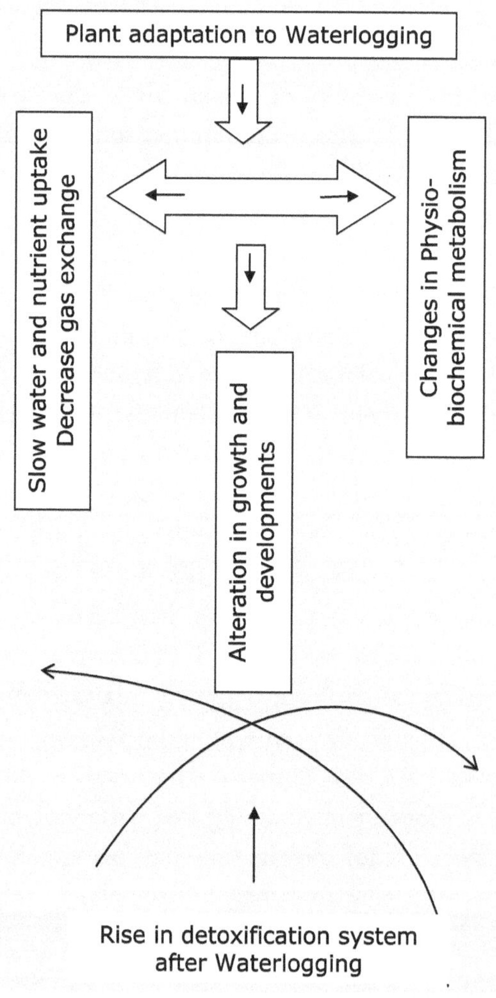

17. Plant response to Waterlogging and its detoxification after Waterlogging stress.

CHAPTER FIFTEEN

Mineral Nutrients - a response in Plants

A plant needs roots in order to grow. With man it is the other way around: only when he grows does he have roots and feels at home in the world.

– Eric Hoffer,
"Reflections on the Human Condition"

Mineral nutrients are essential for the normal growth and development of plants. Plant growth, development and yield are influenced by 17 essential elements (Hopkins and Hüner 2004). Plants may be subjected to nutrient stress due to several factors, such as the negligence of the farmer, leading to nutrient deficiency or an excess supply of nutrients because of the farmer's over-enthusiasm to obtain a greater yield, natural deposits or mining processes. Nutrient stress and associated metabolic disorders decrease plant growth and yield (Lynch and Brown 2001). Plant growth and metabolism are also affected by heavy metal and salinity stress. The development of nutrient stress tolerance in crop plants may help to extend agriculture to unexplored harsh and nutrient-poor soils (Cobbet 2000, Clemens 2001). Nutrients are essential for the normal growth and development of plants. The nutrient requirements of a plant can be roughly assessed according to the inorganic composition of the plant. An idea of the elemental composition with relative levels of each of the nutrients of higher plants is indicated [18]. Plant species may vary not only in the rate at which they absorb an available nutrient but also in the manner by which they distribute that element spatially within their bodies. As a result, the performance of plants as a function of crop yield or plant biomass may be unfavourably affected by stress - induced nutritional disorders. Hence, ROS assembly in roots is observed in response to the deprivation of several macronutrients and may be an important component in signalling nutrient deprivation in plants.

Nutrient stress may result from either low levels of availability of an element or the presence of excess concentrations. In some cases the presence of one element in excess concentrations may induce deficiency in another element. Visual deficiency symptoms provide a valuable basis for assessing the nutritional status of a plant. Plants need a number of essential nutrient elements to carry out their life cycles. Mineral nutrients are mainly acquired by roots from the rhizosphere and are later distributed to shoots. To cope with nutrient limitations, plants have usually developed a set of detailed responses consisting of sensory mechanisms and signalling processes to perceive and adapt to external nutrient availability. The root is the main mineral nutrient uptake organ of plants, and its growth certainly affects nutrient uptake and transport. The micronutrients taken up by plants depend largely on root activities, which influence the root characteristics that control the uptake rate of nutrients. Both plants and rhizosphere microorganisms are known to release low-molecular weight organic acids (LMWOAs) to increase mineral nutrient solubility through acidification and the creation of organic mineral complexes (Lombnaes et al 2002). Several nutripriming techniques are generally used by seed companies in the process of seed production and preparation for growers. Among them, broad-spectrum nutrient seed priming (BSN) is based on imbibing seeds with a mixture of minerals, such as zinc, copper, molybdenum, and phosphorus, which has been proven to fertilize the seed and help provide nutrients for the early hours of growth, completely affecting germination, seedling vigour, and root system development. The soil water content also influences nutrient movement from roots to the aboveground parts of plants. The oversupply of water may lead to nutrient loss by leaching, while a lack of water may cause a high nutrient concentration in the soil, which may lead to problems for crops in terms of obtaining water and nutrients, and even cause plants to die before grain filling.

Deficiency symptoms are the consequence of metabolic disturbances at various stages of plant growth. Nutrient deficiency symptoms in plants vary from species to species and from element to element. Plant analysis is an important diagnostic tool for assessing nutritional disorders and monitoring nutrient levels. Soil and plant analysis according to appropriate techniques, such as atomic absorption spectrophotometry (AAS) and inductively coupled plasma atomic emission spectroscopy (ICP-AES) could provide accurate data on the levels of nutrients that are sufficient for plant growth and development. Under nutrient deficiency conditions, some secondary metabolite compounds are produced in plants. Phenolic compounds are some of these compounds that could lead to the diagnosis of plant nutrient deficiency disorder complications. An unsuitable combination of nutrients in plants could have detrimental effects; the worst situation is a negative interaction. For example, the oversupply of water and N may delay crop maturation by encouraging excessive vegetative growth, followed by the weakening of stems and subsequent lodging, in addition to wasting water and N through excess uptake and overconsumption. Crops have diverse requirements and sensitivity to water and nutrients at different growth stages, and the input of water and nutrients at diverse stages will therefore have different effects. Recently, it has been described that at the early stages of crop growth, a lack of water resulted in a compensatory effect, and crop growth, the photosynthetic rate, osmotic adaptation ability, the water-holding capability of plant cells, energy metabolism, and physiological synthesis were all enhanced after the water supply was restored after a dry spell, constrasting with what occurred when a high water supply was continuosly maintained. As such, soil is the fundamental medium for plant growth and represents a significant pool for the supply of water and nutrients to plants. It is the soil that can alter nutrient and water forms and availability and through which the roles of water and nutrients can be displayed. Consequently, the results of water and nutrient input are closely related with soil properties. Nutrient input is important for crop production on dry lands. The addition of fertilizers, particularly organic fertilizers, can improve soil organic matter, increase the soil water storage capacity, encourage root growth, increase root length, and cause roots to absorb more water from deep soil layers, thus increasing plant tolerance to drought and improving plant physiological activities such as plant water status, osmotic pressure regulation, the activity of nitrate reductase in plant leaves, and photosynthesis and transpiration intensity but decreasing evaporation. All these factors assist plants in absorbing water and nutrients thus optimizing their use efficiency. Therefore, a sufficient supply of water and nutrients can increase the organization of both and cause a good interaction.

Nutrients/elements	Available forms and contents
Iron	Fe^{2+} & Fe^{3+} (2,50,000 ppm)
Chlorine	C^{l-} (3.00 μmol g^{-1} DM)
Sulphur	SO_4^{2-} (0.04%)
Phosphorus	H_2PO^{4-} (0.1%)
Magnesium	Mg^{2+} (0.05%)
Calcium	Ca^{2+} (0.5%)
Potassium	K^+ (2.0%)
Nitrogen	NO_3^- & NH_4^+ (1000 μmolg^{-1} DM)
Copper	Cu^+ & Cu^{2+} (5 – 50 ppm)
Zinc	Zn^{2+} (10 – 30 ppm)
Molybdenum	MoO_4^{2-} (0.2 – 2.0 ppm)
Nickel	Ni^{2+} (< 100 ppm)
Manganese	Mn^{2+} (200 – 300 ppm)

18. Different forms and contents of Nutrients/elements in soil.

Their slow growth rates and low nutrient demands provide late-successional plant species to survive under low nutrient supply rates. These approaches may also assist in the resumption of growth in the plants following episodic nutrient stress periods, which can terminate the normal seasonal growth of faster-growing species in natural environments. However, in some tropical rain forests, large leaf areas and the development of shallow root mats are a few characteristic adaptations safeguarding the supply of nutrients in an environment where high humidity may limit transpiration and the leaching of nutrients as a result of plentiful rainfall is severe in some areas (Jordan and Herrera 1981). Although morphological adjustment can help plants obtain and maintain nutrients under surroundings with low nutrient availability, physiological adaptations can improve the effectiveness of nutrient use in biomass production and ultimately alter plant tolerance or response to high or low Ca supplies. The mutual effects of variations in a wide range of other nutrient elements and toxic metals that are significantly influenced by soil acidity levels make the isolation of Ca-specific adaptations difficult. Given the low concentrations at which Ca can disturb cellular physio-biochemical processes in higher plants, this would appear to be a strategy that allows decay fungi to eliminate the large quantities of Ca encountered in digested substrate. Vitousek (1982) expanded the concept of the nutrient-use efficiency (NUE) of leaf litter as a measure of the capacity of diverse forest types to increase foliar biomass production per unit of nutrient mass under conditions where the total nutrient uptake and return in litter is reduced, thus concluding that increases in NUE at low nutrient-supply rates that increase the physiological effectiveness of the use of N, P and Ca occurred as a physiological adjustment to low nutrient supply in plants.

CHAPTER SIXTEEN

Freezing in Plants

Confidence is not a wilted plant that can be brought back to life with a bit of water. It is a highly flammable object. Doubt sets it aflame and destroys it irreparably

– Michele Halberstadt, *"The Pianist in the Dark"*

In general, as winter approaches, many plants acquire freezing tolerance during exposure to low, non-freezing temperatures during the cold acclimation process. The acclimation process, which induces freezing tolerance in certain plant species is essential and often associated with a period of slow growth and dormancy. Forage legume breeders have emphasized the importance of temperature resistance, especially cold adaptation, in crown-forming perennials such as alfalfa (*Medicago sativa*). Inadvertently however, the improved productivity under these conditions may be at the expense of winter hardiness (Beuselinck et al. 1994). In alfalfa, specific cold acclimation or CAS genes are expressed and metabolic changes occur (Monroy and Dhindsa 1995). Vegetative storage proteins (VSPs) play adaptive roles in plant tolerance against freezing tolerance likely due to their antifreeze activity (Dhont et al. 2006). These VSPs are also preferentially mobilized during alfalfa shoot growth in the spring or during regrowth after defoliation in the summer (Justes et al. 2002). Alfalfa genotypes selected for earlier autumn dormancy also showed a positive relationship between reduced winter injury and high total soluble protein (TSP) concentrations in the roots (Cunningham et al. 1998). The accumulation of endogenous carbon (C) and nitrogen (N) reserves in the roots of perennial alfalfa during autumn acclimation has an influence on the capacity of the plant to withstand winter stresses (McKenzie et al. 1988, Volenec et al. 2002) and the regrowth vigour during the following spring (Dhont et al. 2006). These findings provide insights into the likely mechanisms of cold acclimation and freezing tolerance in alfalfa (*M. sativa*). The greatest agronomic problem in nature is freezing tolerance, as seen in some winter cereals and hardy trees. Plants generally do not grow at freezing temperatures, but they can stay alive at such temperatures in an inactive state and recuperate when the temperature returns to normal conditions.

Freezing tolerance at the subcellular level may be influenced by the capacity to detoxify activated forms of oxygen (Bridger et al. 1994). The changes in the majority of the antioxidant enzymes investigated suggest that they may play an important function in the improvement of frost tolerance in cereals. However, the responses of these enzymes to hardening conditions are different in various species.

From a practical perspective, molecular markers targeting cold-inducible or cold-responsive genes can also be useful in breeding applications for cold tolerance. For example, a polymorphism in a cold-inducible dehydrin (highly hydrophilic protein) increased in frequency as a response to recurrent selection for superior freezing tolerance in alfalfa (Remus-Borel et al. 2010). The progenies from crosses between contrasting genotypes also differed in their tolerance to subfreezing temperatures. Tetraploid alfalfa populations recurrently selected for superior freezing tolerance using an indoor screening method (Castonguay et al. 2009) included positive alleles that enabled the identification of trait-related sequences with potential value for the selection of tolerance to subfreezing temperatures in alfalfa (*M. sativa*) (Castonguay et al. 2012). Although efforts to improve winter injury have been achieved and captured in more winter-tolerant cultivars, cold tolerance can also be affected by crop management strategies. Ice generally forms first within the intercellular spaces and in the xylem vessels, along which the ice can quickly spread. However, this ice formation is not lethal to hardy plants, and the tissue recovers fully if warmed. However, when plants are exposed to freezing temperatures for an extended period, the growth of extracellular ice crystals leads to the physical destruction of membranes and excess dehydration. During quick freezing, the protoplast, including the vacuole, may supercool; that is, the cellular water remains liquid because of its solute content, even at temperatures several degrees below its theoretical freezing point. Several specialized plant proteins, termed antifreeze proteins, limit the growth of ice crystals through a mechanism independent of lowering the freezing point of water. Finally, the synthesis of these antifreeze proteins is induced by cold temperatures.

In nature, cold acclimation is initiated by a combination of the shortening of the photoperiod, which results in growth cessation, and temperatures less than 10 °C. Some species are more sensitive to low temperatures than others. For example winter rye (*Secale cereale*) showed increased in freezing tolerance when exposed to 10 ºC, whereas winter wheat (*Triticum aestivum*) required 7 ºC to initiate cold acclimation. In contrast, spring wheat did not increase in freezing tolerance until exposed to 4 ºC. Thus, there are apparent differences in the response to low-temperature signalling. However, the plant will not achieve the same level of freezing tolerance as attained by low temperature exposure. This suggests that some genes are specifically controlled by low temperatures. Not all tissues in a plant acclimate at the same rate, and not all tissues achieve the same level of freezing tolerance. For example, the crowns of winter cereals are more freezing tolerant than the leaves, while roots possess only a few degrees of freezing tolerance (Chen et al. 1983). Legg et al. (1983) observed that all tillers of winter cereals did not have the same LT50. The point we are trying to establish here is that although all tissues in a plant are genetically identical, morphologically and anatomically, they are very different. These differences may impact the freezing tolerance that results from the upregulation of stress-associated genes. While the upregulation of cold-associated genes is important for the induction and maintenance of cold acclimation, it is equally important to prevent the loss of freezing tolerance at non-acclimating temperatures. Thus, the genes for freezing tolerance may be present within a genotype, but the upregulation of the cold-associated genes may not be optimized, and the regulation of cold-induced gene expression may be as important as the presence of any specific genes that directly confer cold tolerance. Artificial cold acclimating conditions can be a major limitation in identifying genes or proteins causally associated with freezing tolerance. Sudden changes in temperature can cause a plant to enter a state of cold shock, and the genes upregulated under these conditions may be more closely related to drought and chilling injury. Cold-responsive genes are activated by cold acclimation, and these genes contribute to the freezing tolerance of plants (Thomashow 1998). Glycinebetaine is one of several such well-suited solutes with osmoprotection function and is known to affect proteins and enzyme activities and even alleviate membrane damage during freezing (Rhodes and Hanson 1993). It may play an important role in inducing freezing tolerance during the cold acclimation process in plants. It helps to stabilize protein tertiary structure and prevent or reverse disturbance to the tertiary structure of proteins caused by non-compatible solutes (Bateman et al. 1992) and even stabilises membranes during freezing (Rhodes and Hanson 1993). Low concentrations (below 100 mM) of glycinebetaine are efficient in preventing the inactivation of thylakoids at freezing temperatures (Coughlan and Heber 1982). In addition, an improvement in freezing tolerance has been achieved in transgenic plants through the ectopic expression or appearance of a single gene, the CBF1/DREB transcription factor (Jaglo-Ottosen et al. 1998).

CHAPTER SEVENTEEN

Plants response to Radiations

I have noticed that the solar radiation reflections from rippled privacy windows cause greatly accelerated growth patterns in plants.

– Steven Magee, *"Light Forensics"*

The effects of radiation on plants from different sources are now of major concern to plant biologists due to the threat to productivity and growth in global agriculture (Blumthaler and Ambach 1990). It has been shown that UV treatment results in a decrease in the light saturation rate associated with CO_2 assimilation, accompanied by decreases in carboxylation velocity and RUBISCO content and activity (He et al. 1993). The limited CO_2 assimilation due to UV exposure leads to the excessive production of ROS, which in turn causes oxidative damage in plants (Han et al. 2009). Plants have the antioxidative enzymatic scavengers SOD, POD, CAT, and APX and nonenzymatic antioxidants such as AsA, GSH, chlorophyll and carotenoids to maintain the balance between the production and removal of ROS. The effects of IR on DNA create obvious chromosomal abnormalities during either mitosis or meiosis. Plant irradiation augments the level of the most reactive primary free radicals (Calucci et al. 2003). Free radical such as OH, which is produced as a result of water radiolysis, have a short lifespan but are very active and could be accountable for frequent forms of cell damage as well as cell death (Koyama et al. 1998). Therefore, the type of irradiation (for example, either acute or chronic) and physiological parameters such as the species/variety/cultivar along with the developmental stage at the time of irradiation could all differ among studies of plants (Boyer et al. 2009). However, some of the injuries resulting from these effects can be readily repaired and recovered depending on the range of the dose under natural conditions. A standard response to IR in plants is not expected athough some patterns do appear.

The high entry and absorption of UV-B radiation affects terrestrial plants through damage to DNA directly or indirectly through the creation of free radicals, membranes through the peroxidation of unsaturated fatty acids, photosystem II, phytohormones and even the symbiotic association of plants with microorganisms. A number of secondary metabolites, such as flavonoids, tannins and lignins, are augmented at elevated levels of UV radiation; these metabolites shield the plant from UV radiation and guard the cellular components from UV damage. The enhanced levels of UV radiation reaching the Earth's surface due to stratospheric ozone depletion (Madronich et al. 1998) may harm DNA, proteins and lipids, weaken chloroplast function and diminish photosynthesis, growth and development in plants (Jansen et al. 1998). The exposure of plants to high-light conditions and UV radiation leads to photooxidative stress, changes in plant morphology, the peroxidation of membrane lipids and DNA dimerization (Jansen et al. 1998). In some plants, trichomes reduce the absorption of shortwave radiation by leaves and keep them cool in natural environments (Baldocchi et al. 1983). Radiation emitted from cell phones has a detrimental effect on both plants and animals. Forms of radiations in nature are mainly of two types -: thermal radiations and nonthermal radiations. Mobile phone radiation exposure can cause cell injury through reactive oxygen species generation or formation, and cell death (Sokolovic et al. 2008). The radiation emitted from mobile phones affects early growth and biochemical changes in emerging seedlings of plants such as *Pisum sativum* (pea), *Trigonella foenumgraecum* (fenugreek) and *Glycine max* (soybean). Soybean seedlings show variation or a decline in growth and development at early stages when treated with increasing doses of exposure to mobile radiation [**19**]. A modulated field of 900 MHz strongly repressed the growth of and, to some extent, enzyme activity in duckweed (*Lemna minor* L.) in a similar way to that of peroxidase (Tkalec et al. 2005). In environments with intense solar radiation and high temperatures, plants avoid the heating of their leaves by decreasing their absorption of solar radiation (through the production of leaf waxes, leaf rolling and vertical leaf orientation). Short-wavelength UV radiation is biologically hazardous, as it is directly absorbed by DNA and is completely absorbed by the atmosphere. UV causes DNA damage; for example, UV-B causes LPx and membrane deterioration.

19. Image showing the growth of young Soybean seedlings after post exposure to mobile radiations

In *A. Thaliana,* UV-B causes oxidative damage to proteins and the elevation of antioxidant enzymes (Strid et al. 1994). Thus, UV radiation apparently increases the demand for a scavenging system that reduces the amount of ROS. UV-B radiation inhibits isolated chloroplasts. The synergistic inhibition of photosynthesis by UV-B and visible light has been observed in algae and *B. napus.* Plants exposed to UV light exhibit dramatic changes in gene expression. There is a no direct evidence of a signal that stimulates gene expression under UV stress; however, it comes to light that

UV also modifies gene expression because of oxidative stress. Gamma radiation is also used to increase genetic variation in plants and to make them more productive and resistant. Many plant varieties with commercial and agricultural importance have been developed using radiation, such as gamma radiation (Donini and Sonnino 1998). Considering the negative effects of irradiation after exposure as well as the determination of exposure conditions, the radiation dose–response curve and mutation dosages are of significant importance. Comparing other parameters, the level of trace elements may change due to radiation. Additionally, seeds of *Arabidopsis thaliana* that experience high levels of exposure to ionizing radiation produced plants that were more resistant to radiomimetic agents or free radical producing agents than plants grown from seeds of *Arabidopsis sp.* exposed to lower radiation levels (Kovalchuk et al. 2004). One of the effects of gamma radiation is an increase in the generation of reactive oxygen species (ROS). Plants have developed enzymatic antioxidant mechanisms such as SOD and peroxidase (POX) to protect themselves against the harmful effects of ROS. There are three types of SODs depending on their metal cofactors and cellular localizations. Mn- SOD exists in mitochondria, Fe-SOD is found in chloroplasts, and Cu/Zn-SOD occurs in chloroplasts and cytosol. On the other hand, POXs are enzymes that carry out the hydrogen peroxide-dependent oxidation of a wide range of substrates, mainly phenol derivatives (Bowler et al 1992).

Ionizing radiation causes the decomposition of H_2O, resulting in the generation or formation of •OH and hydrogen atoms. •OH is also generated by the photolytic decomposition of alkylhydroperoxides. The DNA of living organisms has been subjected to the damaging effects of ionizing radiation throughout evolution. Although ionizing radiation energy can directly cause both SSBs and DSBs (double-strand breaks, the most lethal form of damage) in DNA, a major source of spontaneous damage arises from the radiolysis of water to produce ROS, including the highly damaging hydroxyl radical (Friedberg et al 1995).

Plant responses to increased UV radiation may vary. However, many plants have developed protective mechanisms, such as molecular UV filters, free radical quenchers, reactive oxygen species (ROS) and DNA repair systems, to cope with excess UV stress (Caldwell et al. 2003).

UV-B stress was shown to delay floral opening and cause a decreased rate of flowering and reduced flower retention and therefore affected the potential yield. However, even though increased UV-B was found to be generally detrimental to growth and flowering, total seed production was actually enhanced under high UV-B doses (Feldheim and Coner 1996). The introduction of a plant system to radiation activates a number of physical and chemical steps between the initial absorption of energy and the final biological injury, leading to the changes in biomolecules and some vital enzyme activities, which aids in the understanding of the mechanisms of action during the early growth of plants for future studies on their influences at the biochemical and molecular levels. In tropical regions, plants are exposed to higher ambient levels of UV-B radiation then those in temperate zones. The reduction of stratospheric ozone has resulted in improved levels of UV radiation (especially UV-B) in the solar spectrum and as a result a large amount of

UV-B reaches the Earth's surface, with serious implications for all organisms.

Plant responses to UV radiation and other environmental stresses have been reported to be regulated by microRNAs (miRNAs). Some miRNA levels are altered under various stresses. The key players regulating UV-B responses in plants include genes such as CONSTITUTIVE PHOTOMORPHOGENESIS 1 (COP1), which is an E3 ubiquitin ligase, and bZIP transcription factor HY5, both of which play a crucial role in regulating flowering. Such photomorphogenic responses to UV stress are also controlled by the genes UVR8, REPRESSOR OF UV-B PHOTOMORPHOGENESIS 1 (RUP1) and RUP2 which act as negative regulators of the UV-B response (Gruber et al. 2010). In a more recent study by Zhou et al. in 2007, it was shown that 21 miRNA genes in 11 miRNA families are upregulated under UV-B stress conditions in *At*. They regulate many genes, including transcription factors and thus control the expression of a wide range of downstream genes in UV-B stressed plants. Therefore, the balance between growth and defence against the negative effects of the adverse conditions of radiation, such as UV stress, ionizing radiiation, and radiation from mobile phones, which are energy consuming, is vital to the survival and successful reproduction of plants.

Epilogue

**As long as I've gone this far, I can't just leave
it after I've found out so much about it. I have
to keep going to find out ultimately what is the
matter with it in the end.**

– Richard P. Feynman,
"Surely You're Joking, Mr. Feynman!"

The daily periodicity exhibited by plant not only differs as a result of seasonal variation but also differs in diverse species of plants. A stimulating agent (i.e., a favourable environment) causes an upward flexure of the growth curve, while a depressing agent (i.e., a stressful situation) decreases slope of the growth curve. The repetitive daily movement of a plant or tree must be due to some daily changes in the environment, either the frequent modifications of light and darkness or the diurnal rise and fall in temperature. These changes synchronize to some certain extent because, as the sun rises, light appears, and the temperature begins to rise. Plant cell signalling in response to environmental changes such as salt and drought and the stress hormone ABA largely depends on the SnRK family of protein kinases in plants. In plants, ecological or environmental stresses diminish the energy supplied by slowing down photosynthesis and the energy-exerting catabolic reactions. Therefore, the SNF1/AMPK-related kinases increased and diversified the process during evolution to mediate the signalling pathways related to various environmental changes in nature. SnRK1s are the SNF1/AMPK orthologues that function in regulating metabolism in plants. All SnRK2s participate in osmotic pressure and ABA signalling, whereas SnRK3s are critical regulators of ion homeostasis required to cope with salt and nutrient stress in soil. Many of these stress-signalling pathways also involve the calcium-dependent protein kinase CPKs, which share homology with SnRKs in their kinase domains (Hrabak et al. 2003).

Similarly, other conserved features include the widespread use of calcium, ROS, NO, and lipid molecules as second messengers, although the generation and signal transduction of the second messengers differ in plants. Identifying environmental stress sensors remains an essential but complicated goal for the study of ecological change. Efficient gene-editing technologies, along with chemical genetic approaches, will help to defeat the gene redundancy problems that prevent the genetic identification of stress sensors in plants. The growing positive perception of the importance of various cell organelles during environmental stress sensing and responses, and the disseminated stress-sensing model will also help us to understand stress sensing and resistance, although the integration of signals from perturbed organelles is not fully understood. This might be due to plant stress responses that might have been coordinated with growth and development; it is essential to understand the crosstalk between stress signalling pathways and hormonal as well as growth and developmental signalling passage. However, there is a way plants can acclimatize to intense environmental conditions through the alteration of their life cycles. The capacity to control the stomatal aperture also allows some plants to quickly respond to a changing environment. Some plants constantly amend the concentration and cellular localization of ABA, and this allows them to react rapidly to environmental changes, namely, as fluctuations in water availability.

Therefore, more attention regarding the plant responses to multiple stresses and the crosstalk between different stress signals is required because much stress research thus far has been carried out on sterile plants grown in culture media in the laboratory; in nature, however, plants coexist with insects and microorganisms. The root and shoot microbiomes presumably include many beneficial bacteria and fungi that help plants resist stress. Understanding how bacteria and fungi enhance plant stress resistance should increase our ability to use these beneficial organisms and should also improve our knowledge of stress resistance in plants. This perspective may be particularly helpful as we attempt to understand the effects of the rapid, anthropogenically mediated environmental changes that organisms are currently experiencing. Ecological stresses of both natural and anthropogenic origin can be characterized based on their spatial distribution, temporal distribution, intensity, and novelty (Kelly and Harwell 1989). Reducing environmental stress requires the cooperation of all of society - one of the most critical components in the industrial system. Fortunately, the field of industrial ecology (IE) is developing worldwide (Hawken 1993). The goal of IE is to reduce environmental stress at all stages, during

i.   the extraction of raw materials,

ii.   the processing and

iii.   disposal of manufacturing wastes,

iv.   packaging, and

v.   the reincorporation of thematerials into the environment at the end of the product's life in a non-stressful way, ideally in a way that enhances ecological integrity. The role of the indirect effects of stress on evolutionary change will be challenging to evaluate because stress can have both positive and negative impacts on evolutionary change.

Frequently Used Short Forms

%	Percent
AAS	Atomic Absorption Spectrophotometry
ABA	Abscisic acid
AC	Alternating current
ACC	1-aminocyclopropane-1-carboxylate
AM	Arbuscular mycorrhiza
APX	Ascorbate peroxidase
AsA	Ascorbate
ASA	Ascorbic acid
ATP	Adenosine triphosphate
BSN	Broad spectrum nutrient
Ca	Calcium
CAT	Catalase
CBF	C- repeat binding factor
Cd	Cadmium
Cm	Centimetre
CO	Carbon monoxide
CO_2	Carbon di oxide
COP	Constitutive Photomorphogenesis
CP	Coat protein

CPR	Cytoplasmic protein response
$CuSo_4$	Cupper sulphate
DC	Direct current
DNA	Deoxyribonucleic acid
DREB	Dehydration responsive element-binding
DSB	Double - strand breaks
EC	Enzyme commission
ELF	Extremely low frequency
et al.	et alie (and others)
ETC	Electron transport chain
ETI	Effector-triggered immunity
Fe	Iron
FW	Fresh weight
GSH	Reduced Glutathione
H_2O	Water
H_2O_2	Hydrogen peroxide
Hg	Mercury
HLH	Helix-loop-helix
HM	Heavy metal
h	hour
HS	Heat shock
HSFs	Heat stress transcription factors
HSP	Heat shock protein
Hz	Hertz
IAA	Indole acetic acid

ICP-AES	Inductively Coupled Plasma Atomic Emission Spectroscopy
IE	Industrial ecology
IR	infra red
kV/cm	Kilovolt per centimetre
kV/m	Kilovolt per meter
LMWOA	Low molecular weight organic acid
LO˙	Lipid alkoxyl radical
LOO˙	Peroxyl radical
LPx	Lipid peroxidation
mA	Mili ampere
MAPK	Mitogen-activated protein kinase
MF	Magnetic field
mM	Milimolar
MHz	Megahertz
miRNAs	MicroRibonucleic acids
Mn	Maganese
MP	Movement protein
MYB	Myeloblastosis
N	Nitrogen
NaCl	Sodium chloride
NADH	Nicotinamide adenine dinucleotide
NADP	Nicotinamide adenine dinucleotide phosphate
nm	Nanometer
NO	Nitric oxide

NO_2	Nitrogen dioxide
NPT	Non- protein thiols
NUE	Nutrient use efficiency
$^\circ C$	Degree centigrade
$O_2\cdot^-$	Superoxide radical
OH.	Hydroxyl radical
PAL	Phenylalanine ammonia lyase
PAMP	Pathogen-associated molecular patterns
PAR	Photosynthetically Active Radiation
Pb	Lead
PEG	Polyethylene glycol
Pfr	Phytochrome far red
PGP	Plant growth promoter
PGPR	Plant growth-promoting rhizobacteria
pH	Negative logarithmic of hydrogen ion (H+) concentration
PHC	Petroleum Hydrocarbons
PHC	Petroleum hydrocarbons
Phy	Phytochromes
PM	Palisade mesophyll
POD, POX	Peroxidase
ppb	Parts per billion
ppm	Parts per million
PQ	Plastoquinone
Pr	Phytochrome red

PRR	Pattern recognition receptors
PS	Photosystem
PSI	Photosystem I
PSII	Photosystem II
Put	putrescine
RNA	Ribonucleic acid
ROS	Reactive oxygen species
Rpm	Revolution Per Minute
RUBISCO	Ribulose-1, 5 - bisphosphate carboxylase oxygenase
RUP	Repressor of UV-B Photomorphogenesis
s	Second
SM	Spongy mesophyll
SO_2	Sulphur dioxide
SOD	Superoxide dismutase
SOS	Salt Overly Sensitive
Spm	spermine
SSB	Single – strand breaks
TCH	Touch
TMV	Tobacco Mosaic Virus
TSOS	The Salt Overly Sensitive
TSP	Total soluble proteins
UPR	Unfolded protein response
UV	Ultraviolet
UV-B	Ultraviolet-B radiation, λ = 280-315 nm

UV-A	Ultraviolet-A radiation, λ = 315-400 nm
UV-C	Ultraviolet-C radiation, λ = 200-280 nm
VOCs	Volatile organic compounds
VSP	Vegetative storage proteins
μA	Micro ampere

Suggested Readings

Telewski FW. 2006. A unified hypothesis of mechanoperception in plants. American Journal of Botany 93: 1466-76

Umrath K. 1929. Uberdie Erregungsleitung bei hoheren Pflanzen. Planta 7:174-207.

Haberlandt G. 1890. Das reizleintende Gewebesystem der Sinnpflanze. Leipzig Engelmann.

Williams SE and Pickard BG. 1972. Properties of action potentials in *Drosera tentacles*. Planta 103:193-221.

Yoshida K, Igarashi E, Wakatsuki E, Miyamoto K and Hirata K. 2004. Mitigation of osmotic and salt stresses by abscisic acid through reduction of stress-derived oxidative damage in *Chlamydomonas reinhardtii*. Plant Science 167: 1335–1341.

Wei L, Wang L, Yang Y, Wang PF, Guo TC and Kang GZ. 2015. Abscisic acid enhances tolerance of wheat seedlings to drought and regulates transcript levels of genes encoding ascorbate-glutathione biosynthesis. Frontier in Plant Science 6: 458.

Sokolovic D, Djindjic B, Nikolic J, Bjelakovic G, Pavlovic D, Kocic G, Krstic D, Cvetkovic T and Pavlovic V 2008. Melatonin reduces oxidative stress induced by chronic exposure of microwave radiation from mobile phones in rat brain. Journal of Radiation Research 49(6): 579-586.

Tkalec, MK, Malari and Pevalek-Kozlina B 2005. Influence of 400, 900 and 1900MHz electromagnetic fields on *Lemna minor* growth and peroxidase activity. Bioelectromagnetic 26: 185-193.

Shan C, Zhang S and Zhou Y. 2017. Hydrogen sulfide is involved in the regulation of ascorbate-glutathione cycle by exogenous ABA in wheat (*Triticum aestivium*) seedling leaves under osmotic stress. Cereal Research Communication 45: 411–420.

Feynman RP, Leighton RB and Sands M. 1964. The Feynman lectures on physics. Mainly Electromagnetism and Matter, vol. II. Basic Books, New York.

Lemström K. 1904. Electricity in Agriculture and Horticulture. Electrician Publication, London.

Zhang H and Hashinaga F. 1997. Effect of high electric fields on the germination and early growth of some vegetable seeds. Journal of Japanese Society of Horticultural Science 66: 347–352.

Moon JD and Chung HS. 2000. Acceleration of germination of tomato seed by applying AC electric and magnetic fields. Journal of Electrostat. 48: 103–114.

Lynikiene S and Pozeliene A 2003. Effect of electrical field on barley seed germination stimulation. Agric. Eng. Intern (August) Manuscript FP 03 007.

Pittman UJ and Ormrod DP. 1970. Physiological and chemical features of magnetically treated winter wheat seeds and resultant seedlings. Canadian Journal of Plant Science 50: 211.

Ward RG 1996. The influence of electric currents on the growth of tomato plants. Acta Physiologiae Plantarum 18: 121–127.

Inaba A, Manabe T, Tsuji H and Iwamoto T. 1995. Electrical impedance analysis of tissue properties associated with ethylene induction by electric currents in cucumber (*Cucumis sativus* L.) fruit. Plant Physiology. 107: 199–205.

Kaimoyo E, Farag MA, Sumner LW, Wasmann C, Cuello JL and VanEtten H. 2008. Sub-lethal levels of electric current elicit the biosynthesis of plant secondary metabolites. Biotechnological Programme 24: 377–384.

Zimmermann U, Pilwat G and Riemann F. 1974. Dielectric-breakdown of cell-membranes. Biophysics Journal. 14: 881–899.

Dannehl D, Huyskens-Keil S, Wendorf D, Ulrichs C and Schmidt U. 2012. Influence of intermittent-direct-electric-current (IDC) on phytochemical compounds in garden cress during growth. Food Chemistry. 131: 239–246.

Gechev T, Van Breusegem F, Stone J, Denev I and Laloi C. 2006. Reactive oxygen species as signals that modulate plant stress responses and programmed cell death. Bioessays 28: 1091-1101.

Lynch JP, and St. Clair SB 2004. Mineral stress: the missing link in understanding how global climate change will affect plants in real world soils. Field Crops Research 90: 101–115.

Ney B, Duthion C and Turc O. 1994. Phenological response of pea to water stress during reproductive development. Crop Science 34: 141–146.

Berry J and Bjorkman O. 1980. Photosynthetic response and adaptation to temperature in higher-plants. Annual Review Plant Physiology Plant Molecular Biology 31: 491–543.

Bourion V, Lejeune-H´enaut I, Munier-Jolain N and Salon C. 2003. Cold acclimation of winter and spring peas: carbon partitioning as affected by light intensity. European Journal of Agronomy 19: 535–548.

Stoddard FL 1986. Autofertility and bee visitation in winter and spring genotypes of faba beans (*Vicia faba* L.). Plant Breeding 97: 171–182.

Khazaei H, Street K, Bari A, Mackay M and Stoddard FL. 2013. The FIGS (Focused Identification of Germplasm Strategy) approach identifies traits related to drought adaptation in *Vicia faba* genetic resources. PLoS ONE 8: 63-107.

Khan HR, Paull JG, Siddique KHM and Stoddard FL 2010. Faba bean breeding for drought-affected environments: A physiological and agronomic perspective. Field Crops Research 115: 279–286.

Fitter AH and Fitter RS 2002. Rapid changes in flowering time in British plants. Science 296: 1689–1691

Hedhly A 2011. Sensitivity of flowering plant gametophytes to temperature fluctuations. Environmental and Experimental Botany 74: 9–16.

Sage TL, Bagha S, Lundsgaard-Nielsen V, Branch HA, Sultmanis S and Sage RF 2015. The effect of high temperature stress on male and female reproduction in plants. Field Crop Research 182: 30–42.

Bienert GP, Møller ALB, Kristiansen KA, Schulz A, Møller IM, Schjoerring JK and Jahn TP 2007. Specific aquaporins facilitate the diffusion of hydrogen peroxide across membranes. Journal of Biological Chemistry 282: 1183–1192.

Sharkey TD 2005. Effects of moderate heat stress on photosynthesis: importance of thylakoid reactions, rubisco deactivation, reactive oxygen species, and thermotolerance provided by isoprene. Plant, Cell and Environment 28: 269-277.

Ryan MG 2011. Tree responses to drought. Tree Physiology 31: 237-239.

Samuelson LJ and Teskey RO 1991. Net photosynthesis and leaf conductance of loblolly pine seedlings in 2 and 21% oxygen as influenced by irradiance, temperature and provenance. Tree Physiology 8: 205-211.

DiPaola JM 1984. Syringing effects on the canopy temperatures of bentgrass greens. Agronomy Journal 76: 951-953.

Calatayud A, Gorbe E, Roca D and Martinez PF 2008. Effect of two nutrient solution temperatures on nitrate uptake, nitrate reductase activity, NH4+ concentration and chlorophyll a fluorescence in rose plants. Environmental and Experimental Botany 64:65-74.

Nakano Y, Higuchi Y, Sumitomo K and Hisamatsu T 2013. Flowering retardation by high temperature in chrysanthemums: involvement of FLOWERING LOCUS T-like 3 gene repression. Journal of Experimental Botany 64: 909–920.

Yeh CH, Kaplinsky NJ, Hu C and Charng YY 2012. Some like it hot, some like it warm: phenotyping to explore thermotolerance diversity. Plant Science 195: 10–23.

Su Z, Ma X, Guo H, Sukiran NL, Guo B, Assmann SM and Ma H 2013. Flower development under drought stress: morphological and transcriptomic analyses reveal acute responses and long-term acclimation in Arabidopsis. The Plant Cell 25: 3785–3807.

Kooyers NJ 2015. The evolution of drought escape and avoidance in natural herbaceous populations. Plant Science 234: 155–162.

Franks SJ, Sim S and Weis AE 2007. Rapid evolution of flowering time by an annual plant in response to a climate fluctuation. Proceedings of the National Academy of Sciences, USA 104: 1278–1282.

Puijalon S, Bouma TJ, Douady CJ, Groenendael JV, Niels PR, Anten EM, et al. 2011. Plant resistance to mechanical stress: evidence of an avoidance and tolerance trade-off. New Phytologist 191: 1141-1149.

Houston K, Tucker MR, Chowdhury J, Shirley N and Little A 2016. The plant cell wall: a complex and dynamic structure as revealed by the responses of genes under stress conditions. Frontiers in Plant Science 10: 984.

Langre E 2008. Effects of Wind on Plant. The Annual Review of Fluid Mechanicsis 40: 141-68.

Wada H, Masumoto-Kubo C, Gholipour Y, Nonami H, Tanaka F, et al. 2014. Rice chalky ring formation caused by temporal reduction in starch biosynthesis during osmotic adjustment under foehn-induced dry wind. PLoS ONE. 9: 110-374.

Huang CW, Chu CR, Hsieh CI, Palmroth S, Katul GG 2016. Wind-induced leaf transpiration, Advances in Water Resources. 86: 240-255.

Schymanski JS and Or D 2016. Wind increases leaf water use efficiency. Plant, Cell and Environment. 39: 1448-1459.

Taiz L and Zeiger E. 2013. Plant Physiology. 5ed. Artmed.

Onoda Y and Anten NPR 2011. Challenges to understand plant responses to wind. Plant Signaling & Behavior. 6: 1057-1059.

Nagano S, Nakano T, Hikosaka K and Maruta E 2009. Needle traits of an evergreen, coniferous shrub growing at wind-exposed and protected sites in a mountain region: does *Pinus pumila* produce needles with greater mass per area under wind-stress conditions. Plant Biology. 1435: 8603.

Patade VY, Khatri D, Manoj K, Kumari M, Ahmed Z 2012. Cold tolerance in thiourea primed capsicum seedlings is associated with transcript regulation of stress responsive genes. Molecular Biology Reports.

Jisha KC, Puthur JT. Seed priming with BABA (β-amino butyric acid): a cost-effective method of abiotic stress tolerance in *Vigna radiata* (L.) Wilczek. Protoplasma

McDonald MB 2000. Seed priming. In: Seed technology and its biological basis. (Black M., Bewley J. D., eds). Sheffi eld Academic Press Ltd. Sheffi eld, UK, pp. 287-325.

Leon J, Rojo E, Sanchez-Serrano JJ 2001. Wound signalling in plants. Journal of Experimental Botany 52: 1-9.

Jaffe MJ, Forbes S 1993. Thigmomorphogenesis: the effect of mechanical perturbation on plants. Plant Growth Regulation 12: 313-324.

Biddington NL 1986. The effects of mechanically-induced stress in plants-a review. Plant Growth Regulation 4: 103-123.

Elliott KA, Shirsat AH 1998. Promoter regions of the extA extensin gene from *Brassica napus* control activation in response to wounding and tensile stress. Plant Molecular Biology 37: 675-687.

Thonat C, Mathieu C, Crèvecoeur M, Penel C, Gaspar T, Boyer N 1997. Effects of a mechanical stimulation on localization of Annexin-like proteins in *Bryonia dioica* internodes. Plant Physiology 114: 981-988.

Johnson SM, Doherty SJ, Croy RRD 2003. Biphasic superoxide generation in potato tubers. A self-amplifying response to stress. Plant Physiology 131: 1440-1449.

Lambers H, Chapin III FS and Pons TL 1998. Photosynthesis, respiration, and long-distance transport. In Plant physiological ecology. Springer New York. 10-153.

Kendrick RE and Kronenberg GHM. eds. 1994. Photomorphogenesis in Plants. Dordrecht: Kluwer. 2nd ed.

Shinozaki K and Yamaguchi-Shinozaki K. 2000. Molecular responses to dehydration and low temperature: differences and cross-talk between two stress signalling pathways. Current Openion in Plant Biology. 3: 217-223.

Niyogi KK 1999. Photoprotection revisited: genetic and molecular approaches. Annual Review in Plant Physiology and Plant Molecular Biology. 50: 333–359.

Karpinski S, Reynolds H, Karpinska B, Wingsle G, Creissen G. and Mullineaux P. 1999. Systemic signaling and acclimation in response to excess excitation energy in Arabidopsis. Science 284: 654–657.

Munns R and Tester M 2008. Mechanisms of salinity tolerance. Annual Review in Plant Biology. 59: 651–681.

Ouhibi C, Attia H, Rebah F, Msilini N, Chebbi M, Aarrouf J, Urban L and Lachaal M 2014. Salt stress mitigation by seed priming with UV-C in lettuce plants: Growth, antioxidant activity and phenolic compounds. Plant Physiology and Biochemistry. 83: 126–133.

Greenway H and Munns R 1980. Mechanisms of salt tolerance in nonhalophytes. Annual Review in Plant Physiology 31:149–190.

Inan G, Zhang Q, Li P, Wang Z, Cao Z, Zhang H, Zhang C, Quist TM, Goodwin SM, Zhu J, Shi H, Damsz B, Charbaji T, Gong Q, Ma S, Fredricksen M, Galbraith DW, Jenks MA, Rhodes D, Hasegawa PM, Bohnert HJ, Joly RJ, Bressan RA and Zhu JK 2004. Salt cress: A halophyte and cryophyte Arabidopsis relative model system and its applicability to molecular genetic analyses of growth and development of extremophiles. Plant Physiology. 135:1718–1737.

Castiblanco LF and Sundin GW 2016. New insights on molecular regulation of biofilm formation in plant-associated bacteria. Journal of Integrative Plant Biology. 58: 362–372.

Niu D, Xia J, Jiang C, Qi B, Ling X, Lin S, Zhang W, Guo J, Jin H and Zhao H 2016. Bacillus cereus AR156 primes induced systemic resistance by suppressing miR825/825 and activating defense-related genes in Arabidopsis. Journal of Integrative Plant Biology. 58: 426–439.

Dobereiner J 1997. Biological nitrogen fixation in the tropics: social and economic contributions. Soil Biology and Biochemistry 29: 771–774.

Belimov AA, Kunakova AM, Safronova VI, Stepanok VV, Yudkin LY, Alekseev YV and Kozhemyakov AP 2004. Employment of rhizobacteria for the inoculation of barley plants cultivated in soil contaminated with lead and cadmium. Microbiology 73: 99– 106.

Boyd LA, Ridout C, O'Sullivan DM, Leach JE and Leung H 2013. Plant–pathogen interactions: disease resistance in modern agriculture. Trends in Genetics 29: 233–240.

Dangl JL, Horvath DM and Staskawicz BJ 2013. Pivoting the plant immune system from dissection to deployment. Science 341: 746–751.

Conti G, Rodriguez MC, Venturuzzi AL and Asurmendi, S 2017. Modulation of host plant immunity by Tobamovirus proteins. Annals of Botany 119: 737–747.

Pieterse CMJ, Zamioudis C, Berendsen RL, et al. 2012. Induced systemic resistance by beneficial microbes. Annual Review of Phytopathology 52: 347–375.

Durrant WE and Dong X 2004. Systemic acquired resistance. Annual Review of Phytopathology 42: 185–209.

Bray EA 2004. Genes commonly regulated by water-deficit stress in *Arabidopsis thaliana*. Journal of Experimental Botany 55: 2331–2341.

Setter TL and Waters I. 2003. Review of prospects for germplasm improvement for waterlogging tolerance in wheat, barley and oats. Plant and Soil 253: 1–34.

Jackson, MB and Colmer TD 2005. Response and adaptation by plants to flooding stress. Annals of Botany 96: 501–505.

Normile D 2008. Reinventing rice to feed the world. Science 321: 330–333.

Stoddard FL, Balko C, Erskine W, Khan HR, Link W and Sarker A 2006. Screening techniques and sources of resistance to abiotic stresses in cool-season food legumes. Euphytica 147: 167–186.

Bailey-Serres J and Chang R 2005. Sensing and signalling in response to oxygen deprivation in plants and other organisms. Annals of Botany 96: 507–518.

Felle HH 2005. pH Regulation in anoxic plants. Annals of Botany 96: 519–532.

Brune A, Urbach W and Dietz KJ 1995. Differential toxicity of heavy metals is partly related to a loss of preferential extraplasmic compartmentation: a comparison of Cd-, Mo-, Ni-, and Zn-stress. New Phytologist 129: 404–409.

Donini P, Sonnino A 1998. Induced mutation in plant breeding: current status and future outlook. In: Jain SM, Brar DS, Ahloowalia BS (eds) Somaclonal variation and induced mutation in crop improvement. Kluwer Academic Publishers, London, pp 255–291.

Savostin PW 1930. Magnetic growth relations in plants. Planta 12: 327.

Phirke PS, Kubde AB, Umbakar SP 1996. The influence of magnetic field on plant growth. Seed Sci. Technol. 24: 375–392.

Chen Y, Li R, He JM 2011. Magnetic field can alleviate toxicological effect induced by cadmium in mungbean seedlings. Ecotoxicology 20:760-769.

Wrzaczek M, Hirt H 2001. Plant MAP kinase pathways: how many and what for? *Biol. Cell* 93 81–87.

Caldwell MM, Ballare CL, Bornman JF, Flint SD, Bjorn LO, Tramura AH, Kulandaivelu G, Tevini M 2003. Terrestrial ecosystem, increased solar ultraviolet radiation and interactions with other climatic change factors. Photochem Photobiol Sci 2:29–38.

Farnese FS, Oliveira JA, Farnese MS, Gusman GS, Silveira NM, Siman LI 2014. Uptake Arsenic by Plants: Effects on Mineral Nutrition, Growth and Antioxidant Capacity. IDESIA (Chile) 32 (1): 99-106.

Van Assche F and Clijsters H 1990. Effects of metals on enzyme activity in plants. Plant, Cell and Environment. 13: 195–206.

Jonak C, Nakagami H. and Hirt H 2004. Heavy metal stress. Activation of distinct mitogenactivated protein kinase pathways by copper and cadmium. Plant Physiology 136: 3276–3283.

Dietz AC and Schnoor JL. 2001. Advances in phytoremediation. Environmental Health Perspectives. 109: 163–168.

Weisberg M, Joseph P, Hale B and Beyersmann D 2003. Molecular and cellular mechanism of cadmium carcinogenesis. Toxicology 192: 95–117.

Gichner T, Patkova Z, Szakova J and Demnerrova K 2006. Toxicity and DNA damage in tobacco and potato plant growing on soil polluted with heavy metals. Ecotoxicology and Environmental Safety 65: 420–426.

Kasai Y, Kato M, Aoyama J and Hyodo H 1998. Ethylene production and increase in 1-amino-cyclopropane-1-carboxylate oxidase activity during senescence of broccoli florets. Acta Horticulturae 464: 153–157.

Pesci P and Reggiani R 1992. The process of abscisic acid induced proline accumulation and the leves of polyamines and quaternary ammonium compounds in hydrated barley leaves. Physiologiae Plantarum 84: 134–139.

Ekmekci Y, Tanyolac D. and Ayhan R 2008. Effect of cadmium on antioxidant enzyme and photosynthetic activities in leaves of two maize cultivars. Journal of Plant Physiology 165: 600–611.

Elloumi N, Ben F, Rhouma A, Ben B, Mezghani I. and Boukhris M. 2007. Cadmium induced growth inhibition and alteration of biochemical parameters of almond seedling grown in solution culture. Acta Physiologiae Plantarum. 29: 57–62.

Tangahu BV, Abdullah SRS, Basri H, Idris M, Anuar N and Mukhlisin M 2011. A review on heavy metals (As, Pb, and Hg) uptake by plants through phytoremediation. International Journal of Chemical Engenering. 21: 1-31.

Nagajyoti PC, Lee KD and Sreekanth TVM 2010. Heavy metals, occurrence and toxicity for plants: A review. Environmental Chemistry Letters 8: 199-216.

Mbah CN, Nwite JN and Nweke IA 2009. Amelioration of spent oil contaminated Ultisol with organic wastes and its effect on soil properties and maize (*Zea mays* L.) yield. World Journal of Agricultural Science 5:163-168.

Millioli VS, Sobral LGS and Carvalho DD 2009. Bioremediation of crude oil – bearing soil: Evaluating the effect of rhamnolipid addition to soil toxicity and to crude oil biodegradation efficiency. Global NEST Journal. 11:181-188.

Honour SL, Bell JNB, Ashenden TA, Cape JN and Power SA 2009. Responses of herbaceous plants to urban air pollution: Effects on growth, phenology and leaf surface characteristics. Environmental Pollutution 157:1279-1286.

Sharonova N and Breus I 2012. Tolerance of cultivated and wild plants of different taxonomy to soil contamination by kerosene. Science of the Total Environment 424: 121-129.

Ogbonna PC and Okezie N 2011. Heavy metal level and macronutrient contents of roadside soil and vegetation in Umuahia, Nigeria. Terrest. Aquatic Environment and Toxicology. 5: 35-39.

Nasrullah N, Tatsumoto H. and Misawa A 1994. Effect of roadside planting and road structure on NO_2 concentration near road. Japanese Journal of Toxicology and Environmental Health 40:328-337.

Smirnoff N 1996. The function and metabolism ascorbic acid in plants. Annals of Botany 78:661-669.

Conklin et al. 2000. Identification of ascorbic acid-deficient *Arabidopsis thaliana* mutants. Genetics 154: 847-856.

Colvile RN, Hutchinson EJ, Mindell JS and Warren RF 2001. The transport sector as a source of air pollution. Atmospheric Environment, 35: 1537-1565.

Saeedi M, Hossein Zadeh M, Jamshidi A and Pajooheshfar SP 2009. Assessment of heavy metals contamination and leaching characteristics in highway side soils. Iran. Environmental Monitoring and Assessment 151: 231.

Feng J, Wang Y, Zhao J, Zhu L, Bian X and Zhang W 2011. Source attributions of heavy metals in rice plant along highway in Eastern China. Journal of Environmental Science 23:1158–1164.

Nabulo G, Oryem-Origa H and Diamond M 2006. Assessment of lead, cadmium, and zinc contamination of roadside soils, surface films, and vegetables in Kampala City, Uganda. Environmetal Research 101: 42–52.

Klumpp A, Domingos M and Klumpp G 2002. Foliar nutrient contents in tree species of the Atlantic Forest as influenced by air pollution from the industrial complex of Cubata´o, SE-Brazil. Water Air and Soil Pollutution 133:315– 33.

Domingos M, Klumpp A and Klumpp G 1998. Air pollution impact on the Atlantic Forest at the Cubataˆo region, Brazil. Cienc Culture 50:230– 6.

Iqbal MZ and Shafig M 2001. Periodical Effect of Cement Dust Pollution on the Growth of Some Plant Species. Turkish Journal of Botany 25:19-24.

Stern AC 1976. Air Pollution Measurement, Monitoring and Surveillance of Air Pollution. 3rd ed. New York, NY: Academic Press.

Erdal S and Demirtas A 2010. Effects of cement flue dust from a cement factory on stress parameters and diversity of aquatic plants. Toxicology and Industrial Health 26: 339–343.

Mutlu S, Atici O and Kaya Y 2009. Effect of cement dust on the diversity and the antioxidant enzyme activities of plants growing around a cement factory. Fresenius Environmental Bulletin 18: 1823–1827.

Kelly JR and Harwell MA 1989. Indicators of ecosystem response and recovery. In: Levin SA, Harwell MA, Kelly JR, and Kimball KD (eds.) Ecotoxicology: Problems and Approaches, pp. 9–35. New York: Springer-Verlag.

Hawken P 1993. The Ecology of Commerce. New York: Harper Collins.

Beuselinck, PR, Bouton JH, Lamp WO, Matches AG, McCaslin MH, Nelson CJ, Rhodes LH, Sheaffer CC and Volenec JJ 1994. Improving legume persistence in forage crop systems. J. Prod. Agric. 7: 311–322.

Monroy AF and Dhindsa RS 1995. Low temperature signal transduction: The induction of cold acclimation-specific genes of alfalfa by calcium at 25°C. Plant Cell. 7: 321-331.

Dhont C, Castonguay Y, Avice JC and Chalifour FP 2006. VSP accumulation and cold-inducible gene expression during autumn hardening and overwintering of alfalfa. J. Exp. Bot. 57: 2325–2337.

Cunningham SM, Volenec JJ and Teuber LR 1998. Plant survival and root and bud composition of alfalfa populations selected for contrasting fall dormancy. Crop Sci. 38: 962–969.

McKenzie JS, Paquin R and Duke SH 1988. Cold and heat tolerance. In: Alfalfa and Alfalfa Improvement. Hanson, A. A. et al., Eds., ASA-CSSASSSA, Madison, WI.

Volenec JJ, Cunningham SM, Haagenson DM, Berg WK, Joern BC, andWiersma DW 2002. Physiological genetics of alfalfa improvement: past failures, future prospects. Field Crop Res. 75: 97–110.

Remus-Borel W, Castonguay Y, Cloutier J, Michaud R, Bertrand A, Desgagnes R, and Laberge S 2010. Dehydrin variants associated with superior freezing tolerance in alfalfa (*Medicago sativa* L.). Theor. Appl. Genet. 120: 1163–1174.

Castonguay Y, Michaud R, Nadeau P and Bertrand A. 2009. An indoor screening method for improvement of freezing tolerance in alfalfa. Crop Sci. 49: 809–818.

Thomashow MF 1998. Role of cold-responsive genes in plant freezing tolerance. Plant Physiol 118: 1–8.

Justes E, hiebau P, Avice JC, Ourry A, Lemaire G and Volenec JJ 2002. Influence of summer sowing dates, N fertilization and irrigation on autumn VSP accumulation and dynamics of spring regrowth in alfalfa (*Medicago sativa* L.). Journal of Experimental Botany 53: 111–121.

Krylov AV and Tarakanova GA 1960. Magnetotropism of plants and its nature. Plant Physiology 17: 156-160.

Pietruszewski S 1993. Effect of magnetic seed treatment on yields of wheat. Seed Science and Technology 2: 621 – 626.

Maffei ME 2014. Magnetic Field effects on plant growth, development and evolution. Plant Science 5:445.

Savostin PW 1930. Magnetic growth relations in plants. Planta 12:327.

Liboff AR, McLeod BR and Smith SD. 1992. Method and Apparatus for Controlling Plant Growth. U S Patent 5077934.

Legg WG, Fowler DB and Gusta LV 1983. The cold hardiness of winter wheat tillers acclimated under field conditions. Canadian Journal of Plant Science 63: 879-888.

Alexander MP and Doijode SD 1995. Electromagnetic field, a novel tool to increases germination and seedling vigor of conserved onion (*Allium cepa* L.) and rice (*Oryza sativa* L.) seeds with low viability. Plant Genetics Resource Newsletter. 104: 1–5.

Castonguay Y, Dube MP, Cloutier J, Michaud R, Bertrand A, and Laberge S 2012. Intron-length polymorphism identifies a Y2K4 dehydrin variant linked to superior freezing tolerance in alfalfa. Theor. Appl. Genet. 124: 809–819.

Vincze G, Szasz N, Szendro P, Szasz O. and Szasz A 2003. Stimulation of seeds by electromagnetic fields. In: Proceedings of the Bioelectromagnetics Society 25th Annual Meeting, June, Washington, US.

Gubbels GH 1982. Seedling growth and yield response of flax, buck wheat, sun-flower and field pea after pre seeding magnetic treatment. Canadian Journal of Plant Science 62: 61–64.

Thomas B 2006. Light signals and flowering. Journal of Experimental Botany 57: 3387-3393.

García-Reina F, Arza-Pascual L. and Almanza-Fundora I 2001. Influence of a stationarymagnetic field on water relations in lettuce seeds. Part II. Experimental results. Bioelectromagnetics 22: 596–602.

Wójcik S 1995. Effect of the pre-sowing magnetic biostimulation of the Buck wheat seeds on the yield and chemical composition of Buckwheat grain. Current Advance Buck wheat Research 93: 667–674.

Esitken A and Turan M 2004. Alternating magnetic field effects on yield and plant nutrient element composition of strawberry (*Fragaria x ananassa* cv Camarosa). Acta Agricultariae Scand. B 54: 135–139.

Novitsky YI, Novitskaya GV, Kocheshkoiva TK, Nechiporenko GA and Dobrovolskii MV 2001. Growth of green onions in a weak permanent magnetic field. Russian Journal of Plant Physiology 48: 709–715.

Ruzic R and Jerman I 2002. Weak magnetic field decreases heat stress in cress seedlings. Electromagnetic Biology and Medicine 21: 43–53.

Sadauskas KK, Lugauskas AY and Mikilskene AI 1987. Effects of constant and pulsating low-frequency magnetic field on microscopic fungi. Mikologija I Fitopatologija 21: 160–163.

Pál N 2005. The effect of low inductivity static magnetic field on some plant pathogen fungi. Central European Agricultural Journal 6: 167–171.

Hoff AJ 1981. Magnetic field effects on photosynthetic reactions. Quaterly Reviews on Bio-physics 14: 599–665.

Rodgers CT and Hore PJ 2009. Chemical magneto-reception in birds: the radical pair mechanism. Proceeding National Academy of Sciences, USA. 106: 353–360.

Katz JJ, Norris JR, Shipman LL, Thurnauer MC and Wasielewski MR 1978. Chlorophyll functions in the photosynthetic reaction center. Annual Reviews on Biophysics and Bioengineering 7: 393–434.

Radhakrishnan R and Kumari BDR 2012. Pulsed magnetic field: a contemporary approach offers to enhance plant growth and yield of soybean. Plant Physiology and Biochemistry 51: 139–144.

Davies E 2006. Electrical signals in plants. Facts and hypothesis. In: Plant Electrophysiology, edited by Volkov AG. Springer-Verlag, Berlin.

Volkov AG 2006. Plant Electrophysiology. Springer-Verlag, Berlin.

Beilby MJ 2007. Action potential in chlorophytes. In eds. Jeon KW. International Review of Cytology, Page 43-82. Elsevier, Amsterdam.

Monshausen GB and Gilroy S 2009. Feeling green: mechanosensing in plants. Trends in Cell Biology 19: 228-235.

Chehab EW, Yao C, Henderson Z, Kim S and Braam J 2012. Arabidopsis touch-induced morphogenesis is jasmonate mediated and protects against pests. Current Biology 22:701-706.

Smith H 2000. Phytochromes and light signal perception by plants- an emerging synthesis. Nature 407: 585-591.

Foyer HC 2005. Redox homeostasis and antioxidant signaling: a metabolic interface between stress perception and physiological responses. Plant Cell 17: 1866–1875.

Poltronieri P and Miwa M 2015. PARP proteins, NAD, epigenetics, and antioxidative response in abiotic stress. In: Poltronieri P. and Hong Y. (Eds): Applied Plant Genomics and Biotechnology. Elsevier, Oxford, UK. ISBN: 978-0-08-100068-7, Pp. 237-252.

Haslam E 1998. Practical Polyphenolics: From Structure to Molecular Recognition and Physiological Action. Cambridge University Press, Cambridge.

Velikova V., S. Fares and F. Loreto 2008. Isoprene and nitric oxide reduce damages in leaves exposed to oxidative stress. Plant Cell Environ 31:1882-94.

Graziano M and Lamattina L 2005. Nitric oxide and iron in plants: an emerging and converging story. Trends Plant Sci. 10:4-8.

Shi S, YG, Wang YD, Wang LG, Zhang and LX Zhang 2005. Protective effect of nitric oxide against oxidative stress under ultraviolet-B radiation. Nitric Oxide 13:1-9.

Beligni MV and L Lamattina 1999. Nitric oxide counteracts cytotoxic processes mediated by reactive oxygen species in plant tissues. Planta 208: 337-344.

Bohnert HJ, Nelson DE and Jensen RG 1995. Adaptations to environmental stresses. Plant Cell 7:1099-1111.

Strauss G and Hauser H 1986. Stabilization of lipid bilayer vesicles by sucrose during freezing. Proc. Natl. Acad. Sci. USA. 83: 2422-2426.

Csonka LN 1989. Physiological and genetic responses of bacteria to osmotic stress. Microbiol. Rev. 53: 121-147.

Koca H, Bor M, Özdemir F and Türkan I 2007. The effect of salt stress on lipid peroxidation, antioxidative enzymes and proline content of sesame cultivar. Environ. Exp. Bot. 60:344-351

Frank S, Kämpfer H and Podda M 2000. Identification of copper/zinc superoxide dismutase as a nitric oxide-regulated gene in human (HaCaT) keratinocytes: implications for keratinocyte proliferation. Biochemistry Journal 346:719-728.

Conner EM and Grisham MB 1996. Inflammation, free radicals and antioxidants. Nutrition 12:274-277.

Lamotte O, Gould K, Lecourieux D, Sequeira-Legrand A, Lebun-Garcia A, Durner J, Pugin A and Wendehenne D 2004. Analysis of nitric oxide signaling functions in tobacco cells challenged by the elicitor cryptogein. Plant Physiology 135:516-529.

Mesa J, Mateos-Naranjo E, Caviedes MA, Redondo-Gomez S, Pajuelo E. and Scouting DRL 2015. Contaminated estuaries: Heavy metal resistant and plant growth-promoting rhizobacteria in the native metal rhizoaccumulator Spartina maritime. Mar. Pollut. Bull 90: 150–159.

Dary M, Perez MAC, Palomares AJ and Pajuelo E 2010. In situ phytostabilisation of heavy metal polluted soils using *Lupinus luteus* inoculated with metal resistant plant-growth promoting rhizobacteria. Journal of Hazardous Matererials 177:323–330.

Upadhyay RK 2011. Plant-rhizobacteria interaction: Physiological implication for heavy metal stress in plants - A review. Israel Journal of Plant Science 59 (2–4): 249–254.

Wang SY, Kuo YC, Hong A, Chang YM and Kao CM 2016. Bioremediation of diesel and lubricant oil-contaminated soils using enhanced land farming system. Chemosphere 164: 558–567.

Barrett-Lennard EG, Leighton PD, Buwalda F, Gibbs J, Armstrong W, Thomson CJ, Greenway H 1988. Effects of growing wheat in hypoxic nutrient solutions and of subsequent transfer to aerated solutions. I. Growth and carbohydrate status of shoots and roots. Australian Journal of Plant Physiology 15: 585–598.

Kuiper I, Lagendijk EL, Bloemberg GV and Lugtenberg BJ 2004. Rhizoremediation: A beneficial plant-microbe interaction. Mol. Plant- Microbe Interact 17 (1): 6–15.

Upadhyay RK 2014. Metal stress in plants: its detoxification in natural environment. Brazillian Journal of Botany. 37(4):377-382.

Chibuike GU and Obiora SC 2014. Heavy metal polluted soils: Effect on plants and bioremediation methods. Appl. Environ. Soil Sci. 2014: 1–12.

Jones JDG, Dangl JL 2006. The plant immune system. Nature 444: 323–329.

Thordal-Christensen H. 2003. Fresh insights into processes of nonhost resistance. Current Opinion in Plant Biology 6, 351–357

Setter TL and Laureles EV 1996. The beneficial effect of reduced elongation growth on submergence tolerance of rice. Journal of Experimental Botany. 47:1551-1559.

Meharg AA, Hartley-Whitaker J 2002. Arsenic Uptake and Metabolism in Arsenic Resistant and Nonresistant Plant Species. New Phytologist 154: 29-43.

Kovács M, Turcsányi G, Szőke P, Penksza K, Kaszab L, Koltay A 1993. Heavy metal content in cereals in industrial regions. Acta Agron Hung 42:171–83.

Macnair MR 1993. The genetics of metal tolerance in vascular plants. New Phytol. 124: 541-559.

Metzger K 1893. Der Wind als massgebender Faktor fur das Wachstum der Baume. Mündener Forstliche Hefte 3: 35-86.

Mayer SG, Naton B, Hahlbrock K, Schmelzer E 1998. Local mechanical stimulation induces componrnts of the pathogen defense response in parsley. Proceedings of the National Academy of Sciences USA. 95: 8398-8403

Asif M 2015. Chemical characteristics and nutritional potentials of unsaturated fatty acids. Chem. Int. 1: 118–133.

Tzortzakis N 2009. Effect of pre-sowing treatment on seed germination and seedling vigour in endive and chicory, Hortic. Sci. (Prague) 36:117–125.

Di Girolamo G, Barbanti L 2012. Treatment conditions and biochemical processes influencing seed priming effectiveness. Italian Journal of Agronomy.

Fercha A, Capriotti AL, Caruso G, Cavaliere C, Samperi R, Stampachiacchiere S, Laganà A 2014. Comparative analysis of metabolic proteome variation in ascorbate-primed and unprimed wheat seeds during germination under salt stress. Journal of Proteomics.

Farooq M, Irfan M, Aziz Y, Ahmad I, Cheema SA 2013. Seed priming with ascorbic acid improves drought resistance of wheat. Journal of Agronomy and Crop Science.

Gilmartin PM, Sarokin L, Memelink J and Chua NH 1990. Molecular light switches for plant genes. The Plant Cell 2:369-378.

Pike CS 1976. Lack of influence of phytochrome on membrane permeability to titrated water. Plant Physiology 57(2):185-187.

Sibley MH and Anderson LE 1989. Light/dark modulaticin of enzyme activity in developing barley leaves. Plant Physiology 91:1620-1624.

Buchanan BB and Balmer Y 2005. Redox regulation: A broadening horizon. Annual Review of Plant Biology 56:187-220.

Dodd AN, Salathia N, Hall A, Kévei E, Tóth R, Nagy F, Hibberd JM, Millar AJ and Webb AAR 2005. Plant circadian clocks increase photosynthesis, growth, survival, and competitive advantage. Science 309:630-633.

Kovalchuk I, Abramov V, Pogribny I, Kovalchuk O 2004. Molecular aspects of plant adaptation to life in the Chernobyl zone. Plant Physiology 135: 357–363.

Friedberg EC, Walker GC, Seide W 1995. DNA Repair and Mutagenesis. Washington DC, USA: American Society for Microbiology.

Strid A, Chow WS, Anderson JM 1994. UV-B damage and protection at the molecular level in plants. Photosynth Research 139:475–89.

Bowler C, Montagu VM, Inzé D 1992. Superoxide dismutase and stress tolerance. Ann Rev Plant Physiol Plant Mol Biol 43:83–116.

Jansen MAK, Gaba V and Greenberg BM 1998. Higher plants and UV-B radiation: balancing damage, repair and acclimation. Trends Plant Sci. 3: 131–135.

Baldocchi D, Verma SB, Rosenberg NJ, Blad BL, Garay A, Specht JE 1983. Leaf pubescence effects on the mass and energy exchange between soybean canopies and the atmosphere. Agronomy Journal 75: 537-542.

Donini P and Sonnino A 1998. Induced mutation in plant breeding: current status and future outlook. In: Jain SM, Brar DS, Ahloowalia BS (eds) Somaclonal variation and induced mutation in crop improvement. Kluwer Academic Publishers, London, pp 255–291.

Jansen MAK, Gaba V, Greenberg BM 1998. Higher plants and UV-B radiation: balancing damage, repair and acclimation. Trends Plant Sci. 3: 131-135.

Madronich S, McKenzie RL, Bjorn LO, Caldwell MM 1998. Changes in biologically active ultraviolet radiation reaching the earth's surface. J. Phytochem. Photobiol. 46: 5-19.

Darwin C 1875. Insectivorous plants. Murray, London

Thomas B and Vince-Pruce D 1997. Photoperiodism in plants, 2nd edn. Academic Press, London

Blankenship RE and Hartman H 1998. The origin and evolution of oxygenic photosynthesis. Trends Biochemical Sciences 23: 94-97.

Glazer AN 1980. Structure and evolution of photosynthesis accessory pigment systems with special reference to phycobiliproteins. In: Sigman DS and Brazier, MAB (Eds.) *The evolution of protein structure and Function: A symposium in Honor of Professor Emil L. Smith*: Academic Press, New York, pp 221-224.

Chen M, Chory J and Fankhauser C 2004. Light signal transduction in higher plants. Annual Review of Genetics 38: 87-117.

Nishio JN 2000. Why are higher plants green? Evolution of the higher plant photosynthetic pigment components. Plant, Cell and Environment 23: 539- 548.

Nishio JN, Sun J and Vogelman TC 1993. Carbon fixation gradient across spinach leaves do not follow internal light gradients. The Plant Cell 5: 953-961.

Schroeder JI, Allen GJ, Hugouvieux V, Kwak JM and Waner D 2001. Guard cell signal transduction. Annual Review of Plant Physiology 52:627-658.

Briggs WR and Christie JM 2002. Phototropins 1 and 2: Versatile plant blue-light receptors. Trends Plant Science 7: 204-210.

Bohnert HJ, Jensen RG 1996. Metabolic engineering for increased salt tolerance. The next step. Australian Journal Plant Physiology 23: 661–667

Metlen KL, Aschehoug ET, Callaway RM. 2009. Plant behavioural ecology: Dynamic plasticity in secondary metabolites. Plant cell and Environment. 32: 641-653.

Blumthaler M, Ambach W 1990. Indication of increasing solar ultraviolet-B radiation flux in alpine regions. Science. 248: 206–208.

He J, Huang LK, Chow WS, Whitecross ML, Anderson JM 1993. Effects of supplementary ultraviolet-B radiation on rice and pea plants. Australian Journal of Plant Physiology. 20: 129–142.

Han C, Liu Q, Yang Y 2009. Short-term effects of experimental warming and enhanced ultraviolet-B radiation on photosynthesis and antioxidant defense of *Picea asperata* seedlings. Plant Growth Regulation. 58:153–162.

Verbruggen N, Hermans C 2008. Proline accumulation in plants: a review. Amino Acids 35:753–759.

Sakamoto A, Murata N 2002. The role of glycine betaine in the protection of plants from stress: clues from transgenic plants. Plant Cell and Environment 25: 163–171.

Zhou X, Wang G, Zhang W 2007. UV-B responsive microRNA genes in *Arabidopsis thaliana*. Mol Sys Biol 3:103.

Feldheim K, Conner JK 1996. The effects of increased UV-B radiation on growth, pollination success, and lifetime female fitness in two *Brassica* species. Oecologia 106: 284-297.

Caldwell MM, Ballaré CL, Bornman JF, Flint SD, Björn LO, Teramura AH, Kulandaivelu G, Tevini M 2003. Terrestrial ecosystems, increased solar ultraviolet radiation and interactions with other climatic change factors. Photochem Photobiol Science 2: 29-38.

Gruber H, Heijde M, Heller W, Albert A, Seidlitz HK, Ulm R 2010. Negative feedback regulation of UV-B-induced photomorphogenesis and stress acclimation in *Arabidopsis*. PNAS 107(46): 20132-7.

Caldwell CR and Whitman CE 1987. Temperature – induced protein conformational changes in barley root plasma membrane enriched microsomes. I. Effect of temperature on membrane protein and lipid mobility. Plant Physiology 84: 918-923.

Jackson MB 2008. Ethylene–promoted elongation: an adaptation to submergence stress. Annals of Botany 101: 229–248.

Mommer L and Visser EJW 2005. Underwater photosynthesis in flooded terrestrial plants: a matter of leaf plasticity. Annals of Botany 96: 581–589.

Vashisht D, Hesselink A, Pierik R, Ammerlaan JMH, Bailey–Serres J, Visser EJW, Pedersen O, van Zanten M, Vreugdenhil D, Jamar DCL, Voesenek LACJ and Sasidharan R 2011. Natural variation of submergence tolerance among *Arabidopsis thaliana* accessions. New Phytologist 190: 299–310.

Kulichikhin KY, Greenway H, Bryne L and Colmer TD 2009. Regulation of intracellular pH during anoxia in rice coleoptiles in acid and near neutral conditions. Journal of Experimental Botany 60: 2119–2128.

Sand–Jensen K 1989. Environmental variables and their effect on photosynthesis of aquatic plant communities. Aquatic Botany 34: 5–25. Colmer & Pedersen, 2008.

Bailey–Serres J and Voesenek LACJ 2010. Life in the balance: a signaling network controlling survival of flooding. Current Opinion in Plant Biology 13: 489–494.

Salt DE, Benhamou N, Leszczyniecka M, Raskin I, Chen I 1999. A possible role for rhizobacteria in water treatment by plant roots. International Journal of Phytoremediation 1:67–79.

Salt DE, Blaylock M, Kumar NPBA, Dushenkov V, Ensley BD, Chen I, Raskin I 1995. Phytoremediation: a novel strategy for removal of toxic metals from the environment using plants. Biotechnology 13:468–474.

Reimer P, Duthie HC 1993. Concentrations of zinc and chromium in aquatic macrophytes from the Sudbury and Muskoka regions of Ontario, Canada. Environmental Pollution 79:261–265.

Boyd R.S. et al. 2002. Nickel defends the South African hyperaccumulator *Senecio coronatus* (Asteraceae) against *Helix aspersa* (Mollusca: Pulmonidae). Chemoecology 12, 91–97.

Hanson B. et al. 2003. Selenium accumulation protects *Brassica juncea* from invertebrate herbivory and fungal infection. New Phytol. 159: 461–469.

Hopkins WG and Hüner NPA 2004. Introduction to plant physiology. Third edition. pp. 246, John Wiley & Sons Inc.

Lynch J and Brown KM 2001. Topsoil foraging- an architectural adaptation of plants to low phosphorus availability. Plant Soil. 237: 225-237.

Cobbett CS 2000. Phytochelatins and their roles in heavy metal detoxification. Plant Physiology 123: 825-832.

Clemens S 2001. Molecular mechanisms of plant metal tolerance and homeostasis. Planta 212: 475-486.

Pollard AJ and Baker AJM 1997. Deterrence of herbivory by zinc hyperaccumulation in *Thlaspi caerulescens* (Brassicaceae). New Phytol. 135: 655–658.

Freeman JL et al. 2005. Constitutively elevated salicylic acid signals glutathione-mediated nickel tolerance in

Thlaspi nickel hyperaccumulators. Plant Physiol. 137: 1082–1091.

Huitson S and Macnair MR 2003. Does zinc protect the zinc hyperaccumulator *Arabidopsis halleri* from herbivory by snails? New Phytology 159: 453–459.

Ghoshroy S et al. 1998. Inhibition of plant viral systemic infection by non-toxic concentrations of cadmium. Plant Journal 13: 591–602.

Miteva E et al. 2005. Arsenic as a factor affecting virus infection in tomato plants: changes in plant growth, peroxidase activity and chloroplast pigments. Sci. Hortic. (Amsterdam) 105: 343–358.

Franceschi V et al. 2005. Anatomical and chemical defenses of conifer bark against bark beetles and other pests. New Phytology 167: 353–376.

Poschenrieder C, Tolra R and Barcelo J 2006. Can metals defend plants against biotic stress? Trends in Plant Sci. 11: 288-295.

Blackman VH 1924. Field experiments in electro culture. Journal of Agricultural Science 14: 240–276.

Florez M, Carbonell MV, Martinez E 2007. Exposure of maize seeds to stationary magnetic fields: effects on germination and early growth. Environ. Experimental Botany 59: 68–75.

Moon JD, Chung HS 2000. Acceleration of germination of tomato seed by applying AC electric and magnetic fields. J. Electrostat. 48: 103–114.

Rhodes D, Hanson AD 1993. Quaternary ammonium and tertiary sulfonium compounds in higher plants. Annual

Review of Plant Physiology and Plant Molecular Biology 44: 357–384.

Bateman JB, Evans GF, Brown PR, Gabriel C, Grant EH 1992. Dielectric properties of the system bovine albumin urea betaine in aqueous solution. Physics in Medicine and Biology 37: 175–182.

Coughlan SJ, Heber U 1982. The role of glycinebetaine in the protection of spinach thylakoids against freezing stress. Planta 156: 62–69.

Zhang H, Hashinaga F 1997. Effect of high electric fields on the germination and early growth of some vegetable seeds. J. Jpn. Soc. Hort. Sci. 66: 347–352.

Lemström K 1904. Electricity in Agriculture and Horticulture. Electrician Publication, London.

Inaba A, Manabe T, Tsuji H, Iwamoto T 1995. Electrical impedance analysis of tissue properties associated with ethylene induction by electric currents in cucumber (*Cucumis sativus* L.) fruit. Plant Physiology 107: 199–205.

Guderjan M, Topfl S, Angersbach A, Knorr D 2005. Impact of pulsed electric field treatment on the recovery and quality of plant oils. J. Food Eng. 67: 281–287.

Park SW, Kaimoyo E, Kumar D, Mosher S, Klessig DF 2007. Methyl salicylate is a critical mobile signal for plant systemic acquired resistance. Science 318: 113-116.

Volkov AG, Foster JC, Ashby TA, Walker RK, Johnson JA, Markin VS 2010. *Mimosa pudica*: electrical and mechanical stimulation of plant movements. Plant Cell and Environment. 33: 163-173.

Vitousek P 1982. Nutrient cycling and nutrient use efficiency. American Naturalist 119: 553-572.

Jordan CF, Herrera R 1981. Tropical rain forests: Are nutrients really critical? American Naturalis 117: 167-180.

Kadota Y, Goh T, Tomatsu H, Tamauchi R, Higashi K, Muto S, Kuchitsu K 2004. Cryptogen induced initial events in tobacco BY-2 cells: Pharmacological characterization of molecular relationship among cytosolic Ca2+ transients, anion efflux and production of reactive oxygen species. Plant Cell Physiol 45:160–170.

Vera-Estrella R, Barkla BJ, Higgins VJ, Blumwald E 1994. Plant defence response to fungal pathogens. Activation of host-plasma membrane H+-ATPase by elicitor-induced enzyme dephosphorylation. Plant Physiol 104:209–215

Fagard M, Dellagi A, Roux C, Périno C, Rigault M, Boucher V, et al. 2007. *Arabidopsis thaliana* expresses multiple lines of defense to counter attack *Erwinia chrysanthemi.* Mol Plant Microbe Interact. 20:794–805.

Rajam MV, Dagar S, Waie B, Yadav JS, Kumar PA, Shoeb F, Kumria R 1998. Genetic engineering of polyamine and carbohydrate metabolism for osmotic stress tolerance in higher plants. J Biosci 23: 473–482.

Bouchereau A, Aziz A, Larher F, Martin-Tanguy J 1999. Polyamines and environmental challenges: recent developments. Plant Sci 140: 103–125

Walters DR 2003. Polyamines and plant disease. Phytochemistry 64: 97–107.

Thomas T, Thomas TJ 2001. Polyamines in cell growth and cell death: molecular mechanisms and therapeutic applications. Cell Mol Life Sci 58: 244–258.

Lombnaes P, Chang AC, Singh BR 2002. Zinc complexation with citric acid in soils as affected by pH and ionic strength. Presented at the COST 837 Action Workshop, 25–27 April, Bordeaux, France.

Calucci L, Pinzino C, Zandomeneghi M, Capocchi A, Ghiringhelli, Saviozzi, F, Tozzi S, Galleschi L 2003. Effects of irradiation on the free radical and antioxidant contents in nine aromatic herbs and spices. J. Agric. Food Chem. 51: 927–934.

Koyama S, Kodama S, Suzuki K, Matsumoto T, Miyazaki T, Wanatabe M 1998. Radiation-induced long-lived radicals which cause mutation and transformation. Mutat. Res./Fundam. Mol. Mech. Mutagen. 421: 45–54.

Boyer V, Vichot L, Fromm M, Losset Y, Tatin-Froux F, Guétat P, Badot PM 2009. Tritium in plants: a recent of current knowledge. Environ. Exp. Bot. 67: 34–51.

Ji GL, Wang JH, Zhang XN 2000. Environmental problems in soil and groundwater induced by acid rain and management strategies in China. In: Huang, PM, Iskandar IK (Eds.), Soils and Groundwater Pollution and Remediation. CRC Press, London, pp. 201-224.

Ruhling A, Tyler G 1968. An ecological approach to the lead problem. Bot Not. 122: 248-342.

Fernandez JA, Carballeira A 2002. Biomonitoring metal deposition in Galicia (NW spain) with mosses: factors affecting bioconcentration. Chemosphere. 46: 535-542.

Bridger GM, Yang W, Falk DE, McKersie BD 1994. Cold-acclimation increases tolerance of activated oxygen in winter cereals. J Plant Physiol 144:235-240.

Jaglo-Ottosen KR, Gilmour SJ, Zarka DG, Schabenberger O, Thomashow MF 1998. Arabidopsis CBF1 overexpression induces COR genes and enhances freezing tolerance. Science 280 (5360):104–106

Larcher W 1995. Physiological Plant Ecology. 3rd Ed. Springer- Verlag, Berlin.

Sung DY, Kaplan F, Lee KJ, Guy CL 2003. Acquired tolerance to temperature extremes. Trends Plant Sci 8:179–187.

Geraldine L D, Lisa A D. 1999. Water potential and ionic effects on germination and seedling growth of two cold desert shrubs. American Journal of Botany 86:1146–1153.

Okusanya O T. 1977. The effect of seawater and temperature on the germination behavior of *Crithmum maritimum*. Physiologia Plantarum 41:265–267.

Crafts-Brandner SJ, Salvucci ME 2000. Rubisco activase constrains the photosynthetic potential of leaves at high temperature and CO_2. Proc Natl Acad Sci USA 97: 13430–13435.

Baskin CC, Baskin JM. 1995. Dormancy types and dormancy-breaking and germination requirements in seeds of halophytes. In *Biology of Salt Tolerant Plants*, pp. 23–30. Eds MA Khan and IA Ungar. Karachi, Pakistan: Department of Botany, University of Karachi.

Jones I F, Hall M A. 1979. Studies on the seed requirement for carbon dioxide and ethylene for germination of *Spergula arvensis* seeds. Plant Science Letters 16:87–93.

Okusanya OT, Ungar IA 1983. The effect of time of seed production on the germination response of *Spergularia marina*. Journal of Plant Physiology 59: 335–342.

Author Name Index

Gul, 32

Guo, 143, 148, 152

H

Haberlandt, 39, 143

Hall, 54, 168, 179

Han, 125, 170

Hanson, 123, 159, 173–174

Hartman, 57, 169

Harwell, 135, 158

Hashinaga, 41, 144, 175

Haslam, 34, 163

Hauser, 36, 164

Hawken, 135, 158

He, 7, 19, 40–41, 111, 125, 154, 170

Heber, 123, 175

Hedhly, 31, 146

Henry, 19

Hermans, 68, 171

Herrera, 116, 176

Hirt, 154

Hoff, 61, 162

Hoffer, 111

Honour, 82, 156

Hopkins, 111, 173

Hore, 61, 162

Houston, 46, 148

Hrabak, 134

Huang, 48–49, 149, 170, 177

Hüner, 111, 173

I

Inaba, 41, 145, 175

Inan, 89, 151

Iqbal, 85, 158

J

Jackson, 72–73, 153, 172

Jaffe, 48, 150

Jaglo-Ottosen, 123, 178

Jain, 154, 169

Jan Ingenhousz, 27

Jensen, 68, 74, 164, 170, 172

Jerman, 61, 162

Ji, 82, 170, 177

Jisha, 36, 149

Johnson, 51, 150, 175

Jonak, 76, 154

Jones, 54, 98, 166, 179

McDonald, 37, 149

McKenzie, 120, 159, 169

Meharg, 82, 166

Merwin, 45

Mesa, 103, 165

Metlen, 33, 170

Metzger, 166

Michele, 119

Mike, 71

Millioli, 81, 156

Mittler, 32

Miwa, 68, 163

Mommer, 73, 172

Monroy, 119, 158

Monshausen, 49, 163

Moon, 41, 144, 174

Munns, 87, 91, 151

Murata, 68, 171

Mutlu, 85, 158

N

Nabulo, 84, 157

Nagajyoti, 78, 156

Nagano, 49, 149

Nakano, 67, 147, 149

Nasrullah, 82, 157

Ney, 28, 146

Nikolic, 143

Nishio, 57, 170

Niu, 96, 152

Niyogi, 56, 151

Normile, 72, 153

Novitsky, 61, 161

O

Obiora, 101, 166

Ogbonna, 82, 156

Okezie, 82, 156

Okusanya, 32, 54, 178–179

Onoda, 49, 149

Or, 48–49, 149

Ormrod, 41, 144

Ouhibi, 91, 151

P

Pál, 61, 162

Park, 95, 175

Patade, 36, 149

Pavlovic, 143

Pedersen, 74, 172

Scientific Name Index

Common Name Index

Subject Index

W